THE RICH BROTHERS

LOVE YOUR PLOT

GARDENS INSPIRED BY NATURE

We would like to dedicate this book not only to our home plot back in Wales, but to our loving parents Malcolm and Liz, who have always been incredibly supportive and given us the opportunities and confidence to follow our ambitions. Our rural upbringing allowed us the freedom to explore and connect to our local landscape, which has been the main inspiration behind this book.

CONTENTS

INTRODUCTION

We grew up in rural Wales, surrounded by mountains, streams, rivers, lakes, meadows, woodlands and the coast. We were very fortunate to have the opportunity to dip into these incredible habitats from such a young age. Whether it was walking up the Brecon Beacons or bunking off work early to go surfing at the Gower, any opportunity we had to reconnect with nature we took.

Whenever we find ourselves in these habitats again we always have the same discussion: what makes them feel so good? In our younger years before this question arose it was all about adventure, dens, swimming and occasionally getting stuck far from home in a downpour and rushing back to warm up by the Aga.

Now our motives are different. Don't get us wrong, we still love getting lost and exploring these wild places, but we have forged a deeper connection with them. As designers we are drawn to these beautiful habitats, each with its own unique beauty, character and atmosphere.

Throughout this book we have chosen to deconstruct what we love most about them: what inspires us, and how we would replicate them within a garden. Yes, these landscapes tend to be on a massive scale, one you feel you could never recreate, but the key lies in the detail. Each habitat is individual and can inspire us in many different ways. When we look closely at one it's not only the obvious features that are the most interesting.

We've included in each chapter of this book a unique design inspired by our concept sketches with moodboards, planting schemes, construction details and methods also given. All these elements fuse together to give a rounded perspective of each habitat and show how you can recreate the same feeling and character within your own garden.

You don't need to live in woodland to be surrounded by trees, or on top of a mountain to understand how best to tackle a change in level. Every garden is unique. Whether it's a large country estate, a modest town garden or even a small urban balcony, the key is to look for inspiration that is relevant to your own individual space.

For us the best bit of this book is that it will give you the freedom to take just what you need to recreate the habitats you love most. And the next time you get lost in the wild, take the time to identify what really inspires you.

PRINCIPLES OF DESIGN

BALANCE   PROXIMITY   ALIGNMENT   REPETITION   CONTRAST   SPACE

PRINCIPLES OF DESIGN (P·O·D) is a method of using a balance of individual elements to create a unique vision. Combining them is the key to creating a garden that contains high levels of interest whilst also conveying a specific atmosphere and mood.

BALANCE

Balance is formed when all the individual elements within a garden are in a state of equilibrium. There are two basic types of balance within a garden: symmetrical and asymmetrical.

Once you have determined an imaginary axis line you are able to play around with balance. If too much emphasis is placed on one side of the garden then the design will feel unbalanced and your eye will be drawn to that area rather than over the garden as a whole.

For example, in the asymmetrical garden shown in the illustration, the tree in the top left creates an unbalanced weight and heaviness. By positioning a group of smaller shrubs in the bottom right a sense of balance is created.

In the symmetrical garden the same tree is balanced by using an axis line down the middle of your garden, which provides a template for evenly positioning the other trees.

ASYMMETRICAL

SYMMETRICAL

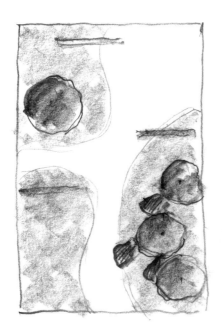

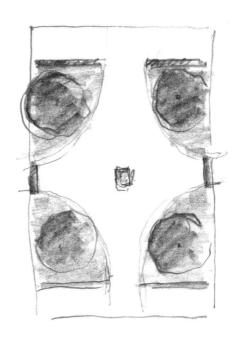

PROXIMITY

Proximity is the process of grouping related items together. Close proximity demonstrates the relationship between the chosen elements, which become one visual entity and lend structure to the design, whereas elements that are set further apart have less of a visual connection and contribute a different atmosphere and character.

The close proximity of stone walls within a concentrated space provides the garden we have illustrated with a stronger sense of unity. Their relationship is more prominent, giving the garden a more noticeable character.

Isolating the individual walls distances the relationship they have; there is still a connection but it is more diluted, while glimpsing the wall at the end of the garden makes the viewer wonder about the space on the other side.

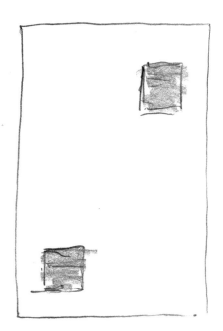

PROXIMITY

DISTANCE

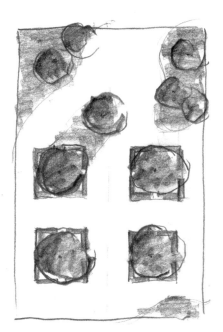

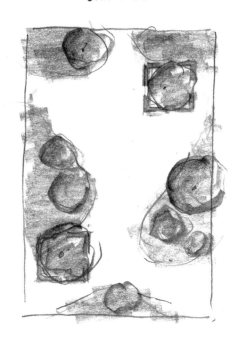

ALIGNMENT

Alignment creates a visual connection between the elements chosen for the design, such as trees, walls and paths.

Alignment between two elements not in close proximity creates a connection that can be so subtle you often don't realise it is there. It's the balance of close and distant proximity that unifies the garden, forming a coherent design where everything works together.

The disalignment of trees within the other garden creates a natural character.

Aligning the trees creates a more formal, uncluttered space and gives a structured feel to the garden.

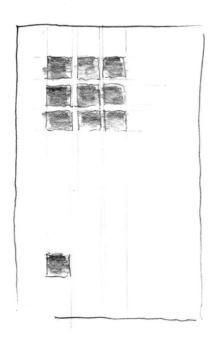

ALIGNMENT

DISALIGNMENT

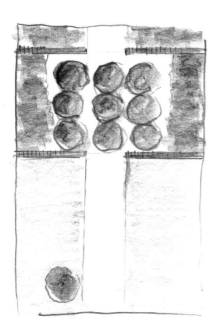

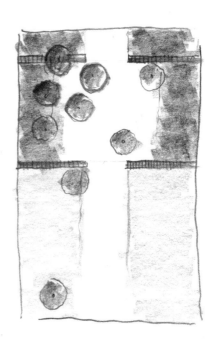

REPETITION

Repetition in a garden brings a sense of rhythm. It can strengthen the design by unifying individual elements, like a thread running through the garden. It can be reflected through form, colour or texture and creates a sense of overall balance and harmony.

Repetition also helps the eye to travel. Repeated forms or plants draw your attention on. This visual journey is another way of creating interest in your garden. Topiary domes provide a strong sense of unity to a design, whereas recurring form, colour and texture lend a more modest, understated character to the garden.

By repeating the same shape in the second garden while using different objects we have kept a feeling of unity within the garden but in a less obvious way. Water, planting and topiary in the same circular shape provide subtle continuity.

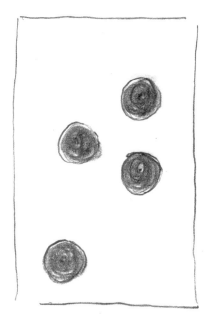

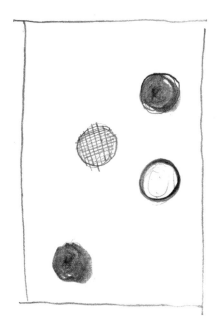

UNITY

REPETITION

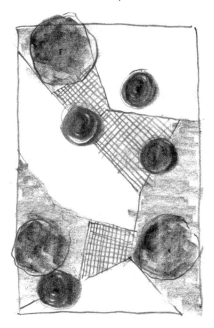

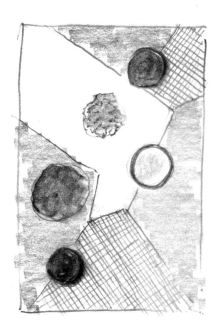

CONTRAST

Contrast plays a pivotal part in the development of a design as it allows you to emphasise certain areas. Contrast is formed when two elements display opposing characteristics. When selecting your palette of materials consider their key attributes and the relationship they form when placed in proximity. Contrast has the ability to guide you though the garden.

By using similar, blending colours for both materials and planting, a thematic scheme is produced. For instance, corten steel walls and brick paving form a strong thematic connection with orange and yellow planting.

By choosing contrasting materials and plants we can create a wider spectrum of colours. This allows individual elements to stand out more within the garden.

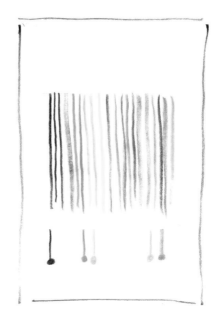

THEMATIC

CONTRASTING

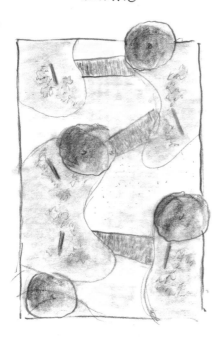

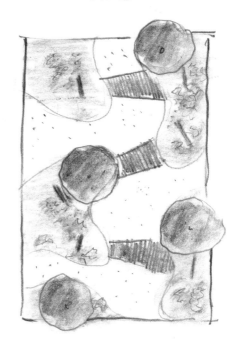

SPACE

Space is fundamentally the relationship between mass and void. It has the ability to change the atmosphere of a garden dramatically.

A void space will convey a simple, open airiness, whereas adopting a more enclosed design and manipulating the available space will suggest more mystery, seclusion and suprise.

The way space is created will dictate whether you move more freely or in a more measured way through the garden.

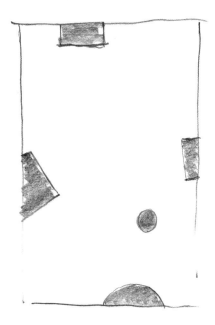

ENCLOSED

OPEN

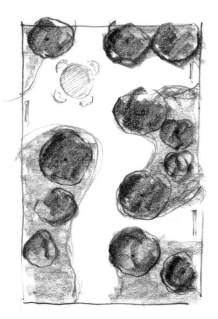

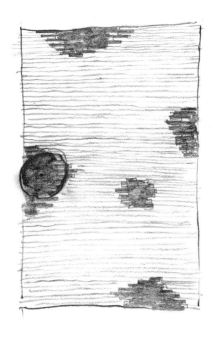

ELEMENTS OF DESIGN

SHAPE   DIRECTION   SIZE   TEXTURE

ELEMENTS OF DESIGN are the building blocks that make up your garden. When you design, it is important to combine as many, if not all, of these elements to create a unique and balanced garden.

SHAPE

Shapes have inherent attributes that bring their own character to a garden. They can be open or closed, geometric or free-flowing, dominant or unimposing. They can define individual spaces or lead your eye from one element of the garden to the next. They convey the design's underlying principles and help create movement within it.

Inside a geometric garden the shape is very structured. Within a modern design this provides a more obvious and direct journey. A central hedge boldly creates a strong division between two separate seating areas.

A free-form design will create a more naturalistic garden. The layout is less controlled and prescriptive. Cloud-pruned topiary provides some structure within the garden but in a looser, less clearly defined way.

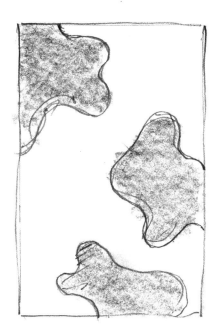

FREE-FORM

GEOMETRIC

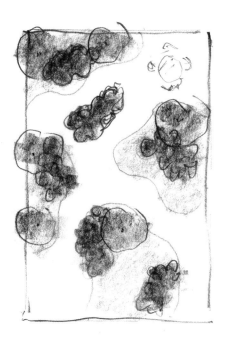

DIRECTION

Direction has a strong influence on the atmosphere of a garden. It defines your journey through the space and highlights the dominant forms. Creating points of interest that continually lead the eye from side to side will make a garden appear larger than one of the same size that lacks these features.

Using hedging and decking to create strong multi-directional interest creates a well-balanced space. The eye is drawn both down and across the garden, making it appear larger. The hedging not only directs the eye but imposes overall structure.

Conversely, by planting the hedges and trees in a strong single direction the length of the garden is emphasised and its width apparently diminished.

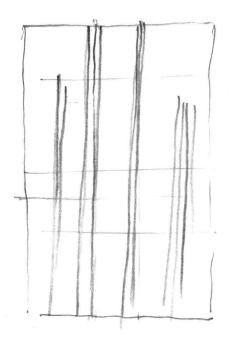

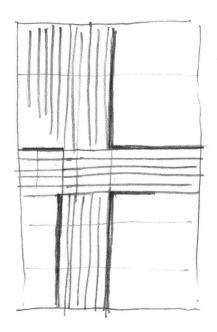

UNI - DIRECTIONAL

MULTI - DIRECTIONAL

SIZE

Size is a very fluid element within the garden. It can be contextualised in relation to the surrounding landscape or confined to human scale.

Repeating shapes and sizes within a garden brings a strong sense of harmony to a design. For instance, rectangular topiary set within planting creates a pleasing patchwork of recurring forms. Having trees that are all the same size also helps to tie the garden together.

Playing around with the same shape while using different dimensions also creates harmony within the garden. The difference is that the variation in size provides the opportunity to further emphasise an individual part of the garden, such as next to a seating area or opposite a water feature.

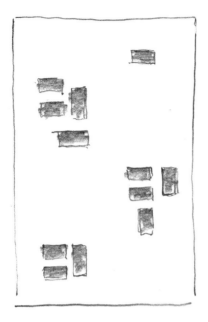

REGULAR

IRREGULAR

TEXTURE

Texture is the surface quality of an object and brings a tactile quality to the garden. Surfaces can be rough, hard, smooth or reflective. Each characteristic has a unique way of working within the garden and qualities that can help to create harmony or contrast. Rough, coarse textures create a more informal, natural atmosphere, whilst smoother, finer textures are principally associated with more formal gardens. Texture can be the actual or imagined tactile quality of the surface. It adds depth and character to your garden.

We wanted to create individual garden spaces by using different textured materials for each one. Wood, concrete and stone are complementary but possess their own unique qualities, which help to characterise a space. Wood adds warmth and a human, hand-worked element, whereas concrete is smooth and more industrial.

Stone is a versatile material that can provide infinitely varied textures. We have used Welsh sandstone in the form of slabs, gravel and cobbles, providing consistent colouring, yet creating very different effects. For example, a sawn slab has a clean, seamless character whereas a textured cobble provides a more rough-hewn, natural effect.

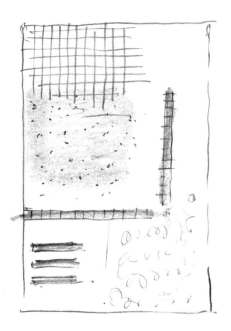

ROUGH

REFINED

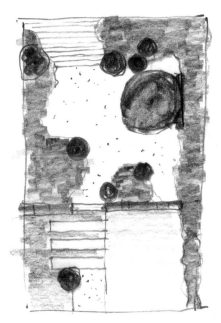

WOODLAND

"Some of our fondest memories are of exploring the woodland above our family house. It's one of the first places we really got to experience the changing seasons."

To us woodland possesses a serene and intimate character, giving us a sense of being alone and at one with nature. When we think about woodland we picture undefined pathways, dappled light and varying tones of green, indicating a habitat that is rich with life.

Strong repetition of vertical forms draws the eye to the canopy above where trees and shrubs merge with one another, creating a formless structure that unifies the whole. It is this balance and harmony that we seek to recreate in our woodland designs.

WOODLAND HABITATS

In woodland generally the trees create an over-lapping canopy, casting shade over the ground, though where some light filters through a variety of specially adapted plants are able to thrive.

LOWLAND MIXED DECIDUOUS WOODLAND

These often ancient woodlands can be found in southern and eastern England, lowland Wales and Scotland. They are comprised of species such as oak, birch and ash, and have a rich understorey layer of hazel and holly. The ground layer is rich and diverse. It may include carpets of bluebells, wild garlic, grasses and sedges.

LOWLAND BEECH AND YEW WOODLAND

About 45% of beech woodlands grow on neutral to slightly acidic soils. (pH 7–4) and can include species such as beech, ash, sycamore, yew and whitebeam. In the UK they are commonly found in the High and Low Weald, the Chilterns, the New Forest, the Cotswolds and the Wye Valley.

UPLAND MIXED ASHWOOD

These woodlands are typically found on alkaline soils that form over limestone within the north and west of the UK. These woodlands tend to be ancient, although ash is a resilient and quick-growing tree so has the ability to colonise new ground quickly. Although they are the most dominant species in this woodland other trees such as oak, birch, wych elm and rowan can also be found.

UPLAND OAKWOOD

These woodlands are found in the north and west of the UK in areas of high rainfall, usually above an altitude of 250m. A variety of species such as holly, rowan and hazel form the understorey layer and bracken and wavy hair grass can be seen covering areas of the woodland floor.

UPLAND BIRCHWOOD

Birch is a pioneering species and can grow on poor soil where the conditions are wet and exposed, unlike species such as rowan, ash, aspen, alder, bird cherry, hazel, hawthorn and blackthorn that are found only on more fertile sites. In the UK there are three species of birch that are native: silver birch, downy birch and dwarf birch. These can be found at altitudes of 250ft+ and are very hardy.

NATIVE PINE WOODLAND

Found growing on infertile soils they tend not to sustain a large diversity of plants and wildlife. Scots pine is the dominant species within a pine woodland but species such as birch, rowan, alder, willow and bird cherry are also found. These woodlands are commonly within the central and north-eastern Grampians and in the northern and western Highlands of Scotland.

WET WOODLAND

Wet woodlands are commonly found on flood plains and on the banks of rivers, streams and lakes. Species such as willow, birch and alder thrive in these poorly drained seasonally flooded areas around the UK. They provide a habitat for a diverse range of wildlife such as otters, birds and bats.

CANOPY LAYER

LARGE TREES

Large deciduous trees typically form the canopy layer. Their leaves are broad so reduce the light available to the lower layers.

Oak	Ash	Beech
Quercus robur	Fraxinus excelsior	Fagus sylvatica

SUB-CANOPY LAYER

SMALL TREES / SHRUBS

The sub-canopy is formed where more light and rainfall is allowed to filter through to the woodland floor, encouraging growth between the taller trees. These shrubs, adapted to grow in lower light levels, tend to have a wider growth form so as to increase the surface area available to absorb light.

Hazel	Hawthorn	Holly	Dogwood
Corylus avellana	Crataegus monogyna	Ilex aquifolium	Cornus sanguinea

FIELD LAYER

FERNS, GRASSES, SEDGES, HERBS

A field layer materialises when a significant amount of light hits the woodland floor. For example after coppicing has taken place. The more open the woodland canopy, the more diverse the species that will be found.

Male fern	Red fescue	Pendulous sedge
Dryopteris filix-mas	Festuca rubra	Carex pendula

Bluebells	Wild garlic
Hyacinthoides non-scripta	Allium ursinum

GROUND LAYER

MOSSES, IVY, LICHENS, FUNGI

The ground layer normally consists of low-lying plants. When the leaves fall and decompose nutrients are added back into the soil, encouraging further growth.

Ivy	Peat moss	Wood mushroom
Hedera helix	Sphagnum	Agaricus silvicola

ELEMENT
SHAPE

Within this chapter we are considering woodland as a single habitat, combining inspiration from both deciduous and coniferous woodlands.

While walking through woodland you instantly get the sense of its wild, loose structure. It provides a feeling of intrigue and elements of surprise and wonder. Planting spreads in a formless way across the ground and over paths, leading you on an undefined journey.

When replicating the experience of a woodland path it's not about the path's shape: the key is to enclose and reveal areas as you journey through the garden

Natural feathered shrubs can be used to break the line of sight and planting can drift into the paths, dissolving thresholds and unifying the space as a whole

PRINCIPLE
PROXIMITY

Entering a woodland you become enclosed by trees and shrubs, providing a sense of intimacy and seclusion. These forms act as a natural boundary. The closer they are, the more enclosed and engaged you feel.

When designing your garden, look to create intimate areas that lead into more open spaces. It's this balance between density and openness that will help to define individual and atmospheric spaces.

Stepping into open glades you feel a sense of freedom. They act as breathing spaces within woodland, and the increased light helps to lift the mood

INSPIRATION

We were inspired by this spot in some woodland. A subtle unde-fined path influenced our journey into this more open, light area, characterised by a mossy, aged boulder. It provided a pausing point in our journey and inspired us to create a small, considered garden seating space.

For us the anchor point to this design is the boulder. We wanted to create an area that not only forged a relationship with it but also provided structure to the whole surrounding space. Running the drystone wall from the boulder creates a strong connection between the two objects whilst creating a sheltered intimate environment. Positioning a few bushy, multi-stemmed shrubs close by helps to blend the space with its surroundings.

BOULDERS

SHRUB
LAYER

DRY STONE WALL

UNDEFINED PATH

Isolating individual colours within a woodland habitat helps to inspire colour schemes within your garden. This photograph provides a beautiful range of deep, atmospheric colours that could be used to inspire the tones of slabs and cobbles, the deep green of an enclosing boundary hedge or accents of soft white flowers.

DESIGN CONCEPTS

INSPIRED BY BOULDERS

It's more common than not to see boulders in the woodlands back home in Wales, large pieces of stone nestled into the landscape, often mossed over with ferns and grass softening the hard edges. Boulders capture the history of the landscape and complement the vertical form of the surrounding trees.

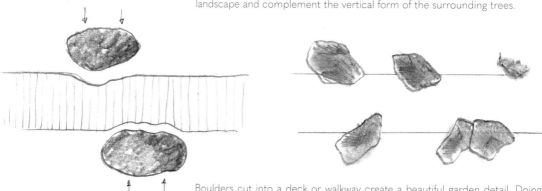

Boulders cut into a deck or walkway create a beautiful garden detail. Doing this forges a connection between the two materials, influences the direction in which you walk and provides a focus of interest. We have used this feature often in our designs and it adds a unique quality to a garden.

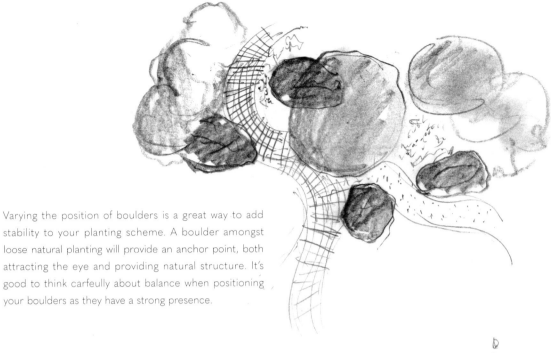

Varying the position of boulders is a great way to add stability to your planting scheme. A boulder amongst loose natural planting will provide an anchor point, both attracting the eye and providing natural structure. It's good to think carfeully about balance when positioning your boulders as they have a strong presence.

Positioning a boulder through a stone wall is a great detail. The boulder, of the same material but in a different form, breaks the line of the stone wall, creating a point of interest or providing somewhere to sit informally and enjoy the garden. Position is key. Think about the boulder's proximity to a seating space or surrounding feature.

In Wales we were inspired once by seeing an aged slab of stone resting against the end of a stone wall. It provided a perfect gateway and really enticed you to journey through.

Boulders can be used to break the line of a path. We love using them in this way; it adds a sense of age and a rustic character to the garden.

BOULDERS

Woodland paths are textured and irregular. Using more linear slabs with varied spacing between them allows planting to creep into the gaps and erodes the division between path and planting.

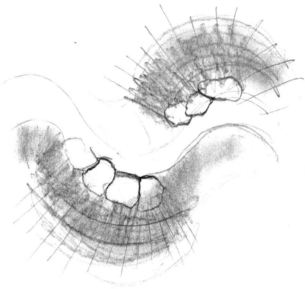

Boulders placed at the foot of a raised path create a natural retaining wall, accentuating the curve.

To naturalise the threshold between path and planting random pieces of stone can be placed on their side. They act as a retaining edge and provide a natural texture.

A seating area within a garden is important. Here we have used the boulder as a support for the bench. It looks purposeful and forges a stronger connection between the garden and its surrounds.

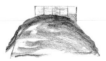

Cubed topiary, often in box or yew, is a great way of using native bushy plants in a more structured way. Cubes provide a certain presence, and, if using yew, the dark green complements and lifts the planting in front, creating a perfect backdrop.

Topiary cubes help to define the structure of the garden. Due to their consistent form they are able to add shape to the space year-round, often catching the eye. We love using them to break the line of a path. As naturally growing things whose form has been imposed on them, they act as a transitional point between the hard, man-made landscaping and the soft, natural planting.

Woodland is dominated by trees, but in a garden you don't always want that overpowering feeling. Pleached trees provide you with the same atmosphere but in a more structured way. The canopy is restricted and gives a more modern architectural character to the garden.

Clipped hedging complements the pleached trees. It almost creates a framed view onto the designated space, a natural boundary that isn't too oppressive and can be used to give a more layered apperance to the garden.

TREES + SHRUBS

Shrubs are endlessly versatile; they can be restricted and toparised or left shaggy and natural. The looseness of an unpruned shrub creates a more natural character. Layering is key when trying to create the feeling of a woodland. Perennials, shrubs and trees are graded back to give interest at each level, whilst forming a soft boundary.

By placing the shrubs behind the feature tree a sense of confinement is created. The soft framework of the shrubs draws your eye down to the tree but it doesn't entice you to walk further away, to better appreciate the form of the tree.

By getting rid of the end shrubs and placing two trees in the foreground with crowns lifted, the view beyond opens up. It's not so much a feature view, more an invitation for you to continue with your garden journey.

Topiary can be very rigid and angular but low-level cloud-pruned topiary provides the same form in a looser, less structured manner. Planting box or yew in large drifts provides you with the opportunity to cloud-prune them into more organic shapes. This process can be speeded up by using more mature plants mixed with semi-mature to obtain instant height variation.

We've placed cloud-pruned box to either side of the path. The bold organic shapes subtly change the atmosphere of the space as you pass between them.

SCULPTURE

Sculpture can create a lovely addition to a garden. Logs are very workable and can be left whole or split to create more angular shapes. We have used them here with steel cylinders placed among them, creating framed views onto the distant landscape.

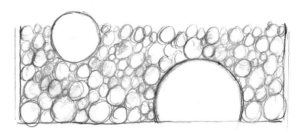

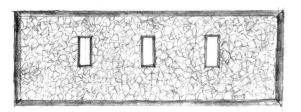

Having more angular-shaped logs set within an oak frame creates a strong, contemporary look. Three rectangular windows, again framed with oak, give a paradoxical sense of neatness and order.

Using large planks of oak as natural 'bookends' allows the wall to feel more earthy, rustic and unstructured. Grading the wall down towards the ground gives it a stronger connection to the land, as opposed to the more rectangular form of the other walls.

INSPIRED BY PATHS

A serpentine path wanders through the trees and shrubs reavealing different perspectives on the garden and extending the journey. When we look to create a more natural design, it's the relationship between the shape of the path and the positioning of the trees and shrubs that is key.

As the land falls away here we have used the decking to our advantage as not only does it provide a more elevated perspective but it also demonstrates a neat way of dealing with the change in level.

A large expanse of deck can be dull. We've introduced a grove of birch trees planted either side and within the deck, creating a close connection. It's good here to pick trees that have a higher crown as this will make a confined space feel more open. Ornamental pear and field maple are two other great options.

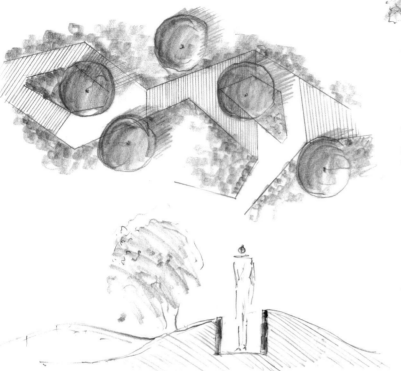

Woodland paths are often curvaceous, guiding you around the trees and shrubs. When planning out your primary and secondary paths, try to create planting islands. This produces a more interesting route plus the opportunity to create more secluded spaces. A change in material, for example stone to wood, will create a cooler-to-warmer character in the garden. It's good to have the option to take different routes, either angular or curved, to add the element of mystery and choice.

Undulations create natural land sculpture. They have the ability to add character and depth to the simplest of open spaces. Here we've cut a path through the mounded land to create a feature path. Shrubs would add another dimension, making a visitor feel more enclosed and connected to the immediate landscape.

Seating is paramount in a garden. Timber provides a great material from which to construct benches. Here we've used the same decking timbers as in the raised walkway, to show how you could create areas for lounging and sitting in.

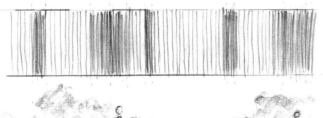

WOODLAND PATH DESIGN

This series of concept sketches shows a single path's progression from wild and undefined to designed and architectural. We wanted to demonstrate how, by following just one line, you can progressively adapt and enhance a design. Our concept was to begin with a subtle pathway and gradually enhance it, until the path started to define the surrounding space.

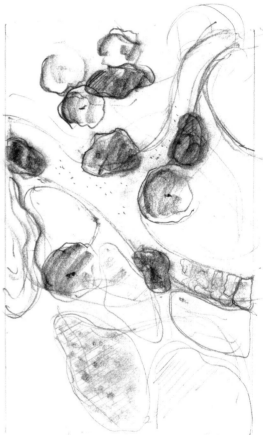

SOFT

Undulations define the grass paths, while pockets of native shrubs create soft screening that entices you to continue your journey.

NATURAL

A gravel path forms a more practical surface, though still loose and undefined, reflecting the character of a woodland landscape. Boulders placed at the edges create a wildness that gradually gives way to the natural planting scheme. The gravel starts to feature larger inset slabs, producing a more designed and structured effect.

MINIMAL

Stone walls rise from the ground, dividing the space. The natural stone slabs are reshaped into a more angular contemporary appearance, replicating disjointed stone paths. As you walk between the walls the large slabs break up into smaller, more linear slabs, complementing the form of the wall. A natural grouping of more ornamental trees and shrubs welcomes you into the new space. As you proceed they dwindle, leaving a single specimen tree set purposefully in the middle of the planting bed.

MODERN

The final space combines wood and concrete with the original stone. The simplicity of the concrete is complemented by the texture of the wood, which defines the route through the garden. The stone walls act in relation to the floorscape, working off the angles to create individual areas that can be used for seating.

A WOODLAND GARDEN

INITIAL DESIGN PLAN

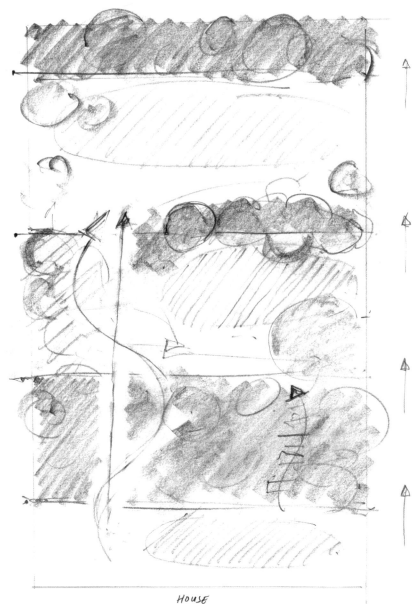

**LAYERED
WOODLAND
BOUNDARY**

OPEN SPACE
imitating a woodland
glade

**IMMERSIVE
SEATING SPACE**
set amongst trees and
shrubs

WOODLAND AREA
dense canopy of trees
underplanted with shade-
loving plants

FUNCTIONAL AREA
directly outside house

HOUSE

When starting to design your garden you should first think about dividing the space up into individual character areas. A character area is a space with a distinct atmosphere and purpose. For example, at the start of this design we move from an open functional area right outside the house, into a dense, enclosed wooded area. This change in material, function and planting density creates a clearly defined progression from one area to the next.

CONCEPT DEVELOPMENT

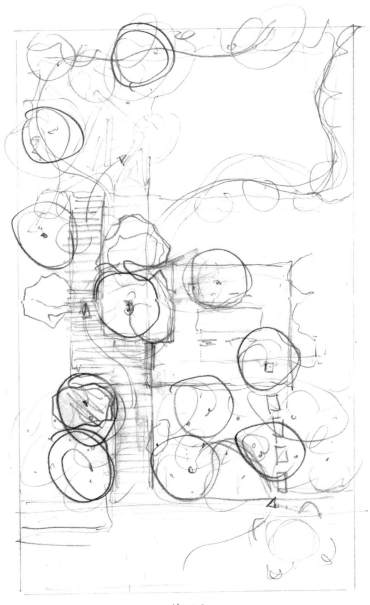

HOUSE

Change of material to lead from the deck on to the lawn

Disjointed wooden path creates a modern yet natural feel to the garden, whilst providing a strong anchor within the design

Birch trees scattered throughout the garden create a recurring motif

Shrubs provide natural screens to disrupt views

Planting allowed to drift into individual spaces, linking the garden as a whole

Trees placed within the seating space, continuing the thread of trees throughout the garden

Tree grove to be unstructured and natural

Secondary path to provide a more considered route

Once you are happy with your individual character areas you can begin to sketch out the bones of the design. Loosely develop the areas into designed spaces, keeping in mind their function (amount of people, seating, dining).

Decide the atmosphere you want to create (open/enclosed/peaceful), the planting surrounding you (low perennials/tall grasses/shrubs/trees), and the journey you take through these spaces (direct/intermittent/wandering).

CONCEPT DEVELOPMENT

Fragmented linear path leads through the planting, echoing the appearance of fallen trees

Boulders mould into the deck creating form and adding interest

The fragmented path links the deck and the open glade

Open glade to be kept as lawn, planted with natural bulbs

Opportunity to use the space for more seating

Two bespoke benches creating a functional relaxation space surrounded by planting, shrubs and trees

Shrubs to be kept feathered and bushy to give an unkempt and natural appearance

HOUSE

This next stage is all about refining the design. Really think about how the individual spaces are going to be used and whether any adjustments will enhance that. Take time over the species and positioning of trees and shrubs as they all have unique growth habits, so will adapt to spaces differently. You can start to develop the smaller details as well. For example, in this design we have added boulders cut into the path, revisiting the way you enter the immersive seating space, its seating arrangment and the positioning of shrubs.

FINAL DESIGN

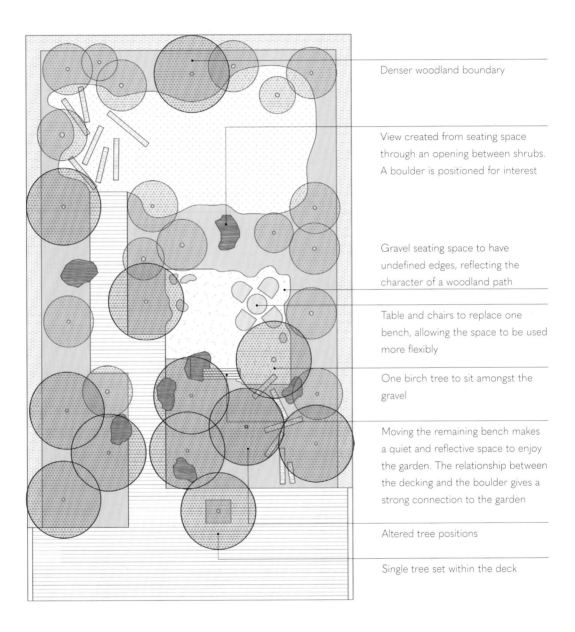

Denser woodland boundary

View created from seating space through an opening between shrubs. A boulder is positioned for interest

Gravel seating space to have undefined edges, reflecting the character of a woodland path

Table and chairs to replace one bench, allowing the space to be used more flexibly

One birch tree to sit amongst the gravel

Moving the remaining bench makes a quiet and reflective space to enjoy the garden. The relationship between the decking and the boulder gives a strong connection to the garden

Altered tree positions

Single tree set within the deck

Once you have refined the details you can start to draw up a final masterplan. It's inevitable that things will change again at this stage as you can see from our design. This plan has been drawn up on the computer using AutoCAD but you can achieve the same level of detail with a pencil, a scaled ruler and a bit more patience!

FINAL DESIGN VISUALS

The section below clearly shows the individual character areas as you journey through the garden. moving beneath the birch tree canopy, beside the intimate seating area and out onto the woodland glade lawn.

It shows the balance between more densely planted trees through to areas that are comparatively open and light. It's this relationship that provides the intimate woodland feeling to the design.

PATH

LARGE DECK   WOODLAND ATMOSPHERE   SEATING SPACE

SEATING AREA

TREE CANOPY

SHRUB LAYER

Looking toward the house, this visual shows the density of shrubs, concealing a lot of the garden whilst revealing the intimate seating space and the path entrance.

OPEN GLADE

PATH ENTRANCE

The birch trees and hazel shrubs create a very natural feeling, combining to provide a golden-yellow tone to the garden in autumn.

OPEN GLADE

WOODLAND BOUNDARY

WOODLAND

WOODLAND PLANTING

When we imitate woodland planting we look to create loose groupings of perennials and grasses that gently blend with each other. Woodland-style planting should be soft, fluid and have a random apperance, yet the plants should all have a relationship to one other. Drifts of planting should emulate the woodland floor where the palette would be dominated by the colour green and soft hues of white, blue and yellow.

Trees and shrubs provide natural structure. They can be used to divide the planting beds and provide height within a garden.

Larger trees and shrubs, such as oak, hazel and birch can give your garden a sense of age, replicating an ancient woodland structure, each providing a different attribute and character that will complement your planting scheme.

NATIVE WOODLAND PLANTING SCHEME

Below are a few of our favourite native woodland plants that also look great in gardens. Each has been displayed according to its woodland layer and on the next page we demonstrate how they can be laid out in your garden.

CANOPY LAYER

Birch Betula pendula

Field maple Acer campestre

Alder Alnus glutinosa

SUB-CANOPY LAYER

Hazel Corylus avellana

Box Buxus sempervirens

Dogwood Cornus sanguinea

FIELD LAYER

Male fern Dryopteris filix-mas

Red fescue Festuca rubra

Bluebell Hyacinthoides non-scripta

GROUND LAYER

Ivy Hedera helix

Peat moss Sphagnum

CREATING A NATIVE WOODLAND GARDEN

INITIAL DESIGN PLAN

Birch Betula pendula
Alder Alnus glutinosa
Hazel Corylus avellana
Box Buxus sempervirens
Dogwood Cornus sanguinea

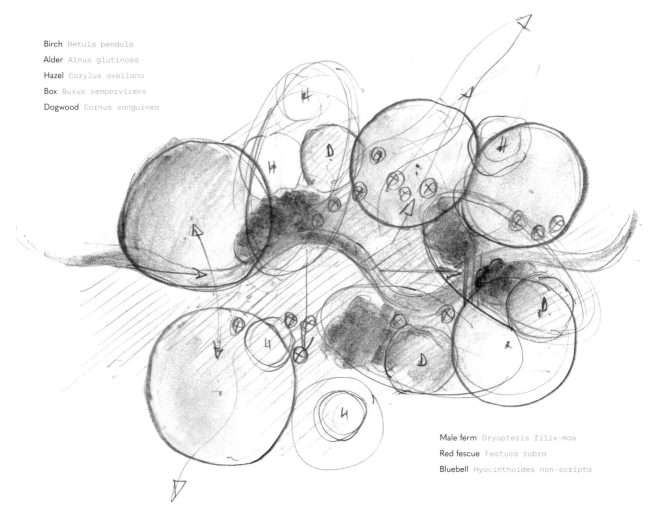

Male fern Dryopteris filix-mas
Red fescue Festuca rubra
Bluebell Hyacinthoides non-scripta

This planting scheme shows how you can use simple design principles to create a fragment of a woodland habitat.

The principles of repetition and proximity are shown with the layout of trees and shrubs, which are positioned in a random and unaligned way. The path provides the elements of shape and direction, and as you journey through the planting you move between enclosed and open spaces.

It's important to think about the relationships between trees and shrubs, whether they are evergreen or deciduous and their positioning relative to the primary path. Your chosen layout of trees and shrubs controls the amount of light and water available in this area, further influencing your planting scheme.

Within this planting scheme we haven't used common ivy. This is because it's a small space and ivy can be extremely invasive. It would be best used climbing up an unsightly building or structure.

DEVELOPED PLANTING PLAN

Birch trees provide the canopy layer. With dappled leaves, bark detail and autumn colour they are the perfect choice to let light filter through onto the woodland floor.

Hazel and dogwood form the deciduous shrub layer. Natural and understated, they provide a muted backdrop.

Natural groupings of evergreen box have been positioned to obscure your eyelines to either side of the path.

The absence of trees within the centre of the design forms an open glade, providing the plants with more light. We have used bluebells and grasses to create a carpet effect that would evolve and naturalise over time.

Ferns have been positioned in the more shaded areas, alongside shrubs and on the edge of the tree canopy.

FIELD LAYER

PERENNIALS

Lady ferm

Athyrium filix-femina

One of our favourite deciduous ferns. Its soft feathery fronds are beautifully understated. A real champion in a sheltered shady spot. Tolerates most soil types and prefers the gound moist but well drained.

HEIGHT ↕ 1.2m SPREAD ↔ 0.9m
POSITION ☀ FULL SUN ⛅ PARTIAL SHADE HARDINESS 3 4 5 **6** 7

Small yellow foxglove

Digitalis lutea

A herbaceous perennial that is a more delicate variety of foxglove. Perfect for giving some architectural form that isn't too ornamental. Can tolerate all soil types provided they are well drained.

HEIGHT ↕ 0.6m SPREAD ↔ 0.3m FLOWERING ✻ JUN-JUL
POSITION ⛅ PARTIAL SHADE HARDINESS 3 4 5 **6** 7

Bugbane

Actaea simplex (Atropurpurea group)

A really striking flower. We like to say it's a paint stroke amongst the planting. The perfect perennial to brighten up a more shaded part of the garden. Grows in a more sheltered spot in moist, poorer drained soils. Prefers clay and loam.

HEIGHT ↕ 1.2m SPREAD ↔ 0.6m FLOWERING ✻ SEP-OCT
POSITION ⛅ PARTIAL SHADE HARDINESS 3 4 5 6 **7**

White wood aster

Aster divaricatus

Such sympathetic leaves, perfect for front of border in a more natural scheme, and then in late summer a white haze of flowers suspended from dainty black stems. Grows well under shrubs. Also tolerates open sunny spots.

HEIGHT ↕ 0.5m SPREAD ↔ 0.5m FLOWERING ✻ AUG-SEP
POSITION ☀ FULL SUN ⛅ PARTIAL SHADE HARDINESS 3 4 **5** 6 7

❸ hardy in coastal and relatively mild parts of the UK [-5 to 1°C]
❹ hardy through most of the UK [-10 to -5°C]
❺ hardy in most places throughout the UK, even in severe winters [-15 to -10°C]
❻ hardy in all of UK and northern Europe [-20 to -15°C]
❼ hardy in the severest European continental climates [-20°C and lower]

Dusky cranesbill

Geranium phaeum var. phaeum 'Samobor'

A clump-forming perennial with a leaf that's almost as good-looking as its flower. A great plant for accentuating other deep colours in your scheme. Prefers a rich, moist soil. Loam, sandy or clay.

HEIGHT ↕ 0.8m SPREAD ↔ 0.45m FLOWERING MAY-JUN
POSITION FULL SUN PARTIAL SHADE HARDINESS 3 4 5 6 7

Fringe cups

Tellima grandiflora

A compact perennial with really subtly colouring. Clumped green foliage with tall spires of green-white bell-shaped flowers. A perfect candidate for a dry shady spot. Prefers a sand, loam or chalk soil.

HEIGHT ↕ 0.8m SPREAD ↔ 0.3m FLOWERING MAY-JUL
POSITION PARTIAL SHADE HARDINESS 3 4 5 6 7

Great masterwort

Astrantia major 'Alba'

A modern classic. One of our favourites for a shady scheme. Great leaf shape for contrasting with other plants and a beautiful flowerhead. Prefers to grow in a moist, well-drained, fertile soil, either loam or clay.

HEIGHT ↕ 0.9m SPREAD ↔ 0.45m FLOWERING JUN-AUG
POSITION FULL SUN PARTIAL SHADE HARDINESS 3 4 5 6 7

Yellow wax bells

Kirengeshoma palmata

Delicate upright stems and multi-layered pale green leaves make this a great perennial for ground cover. Displaying bowing, bell-shaped flowers in late summer, it's a perfect woodland understorey plant. Prefers a moist, well-drained soil. Sand, loam or clay. Will need to be in a shetered spot.

HEIGHT ↕ 1.2m SPREAD ↔ 0.75m FLOWERING AUG-SEP
POSITION PARTIAL SHADE HARDINESS 3 4 5 6 7

FIELD LAYER

GRASSES

Japanese forest grass
Hakonechloa macra

A great grass for the front of a border and planting en masse. Forms a large clump of luscious cascading leaves, which are just as beautiful late in the season when the leaves turn bronze. A great semi-evergreen grass for a more minimal style. Grows in all soil types providing the spot is cool and moist.

HEIGHT ↕ 0.35m SPREAD ↔ 0.4m FLOWERING ❋ AUG-SEP
POSITION ◐ PARTIAL SHADE HARDINESS 3 4 5 6 **7**

Tufted-hair grass
Deschampsia cespitosa

Very tall and delicate and beside a path you can't help but touch it. Fresh green foliage with a golden feathery flower, turning into an oaty haze in late summer. Soft movement in the wind. Great at softening architectural plants like foxgloves. Grows in most soil types but prefers a moist, well-drained soil.

HEIGHT ↕ 0.6m SPREAD ↔ 0.45m FLOWERING ❋ JUN-JUL
POSITION ☀ FULL SUN ◐ PARTIAL SHADE HARDINESS 3 4 **5** 6 7

Snowy woodrush
Luzula nivea

This evergreen grass forms a clump of narrow rough leaves topped with a tufft of pure white, turning bronze thoughout the summer. A perfect grass to plant in large drifts. Grows best in a moist, well-drained soil. Can tolerate an exposed site.

HEIGHT ↕ 0.6m SPREAD ↔ 0.45m FLOWERING ❋ JUN-JUL
POSITION ☀ FULL SUN ◐ PARTIAL SHADE HARDINESS 3 4 **5** 6 7

Quaking grass
Briza media

A semi-evergreen clump-forming grass with an amazing burst of flowerheads. Their soft purple hue combines well with other deep-coloured flowering perennials like dusky cranesbill. Grows well in any well-drained soil.

HEIGHT ↕ 0.9m SPREAD ↔ 0.3m FLOWERING ❋ MAY-AUG
POSITION ☀ FULL SUN ◐ PARTIAL SHADE HARDINESS 3 4 5 6 **7**

WOODLAND MEADOW

PLANTING MIX

Within a garden there are always patches of ground shaded out by hedges, trees and buildings. This meadow mix provides a blend of species that will thrive in part-shade.

PRIMARY SPECIES   <75%

↑ Crested dog's tail
Cynosurus cristatus

Slender creeping red fescue
Festuca rubra
litoralis

Strong creeping red fescue
Festuca rubra rubra

Wood meadow grass
Poa nemoralis

Tall fescue
Festuca arundinacea

SECONDARY SPECIES   <15%

↑ Corncockle
Agrostemma githago

Foxglove
Digitalis purpurea

Sweet cicely
Myrrhis odorata

Meadowsweet
Filipendula
ulmaria

Bluebell
Hyacinthoides
non-scripta

Red campion
Silene dioica

TERTIARY SPECIES   <10%

↑ Bugle
Ajuga reptans

Corn marigold
Chrysanthemum segetum

Hedge bedstraw
Galium mollugo

White campion
Silene latifolia

Upright hedge parsley
Torilis japonica

Ramsons
Allium ursinum

Garlic mustard
Alliaria petiolata

Wood sage
Teucrium scorodonia

Traveller's joy
Clematis vitalba

Ragged robin
Lychnis flos-cuculi

SUB-CANOPY LAYER

DECIDUOUS SHRUBS

Wayfaring

Viburnum lantana

An upright deciduous shrub with broadly ovate grey-green leaves, clusters of small white flowers in late spring followed by red flattened berries that ripen to black. Commonly found in scrub, hedgerows and woodland edges, especially on chalky soils.

HEIGHT ↕ 4m SPREAD ↔ 4m FLOWERING ✻ MAY-JUN
POSITION ☼ FULL SUN ☼ PARTIAL SHADE HARDINESS 3 4 5 6 **7**

Common hawthorn

Crataegus monogyna

Absolutely everywhere back in Wales, especially in exposed areas. A real trouper, puts up with most conditions. Characterful deciduous shrub that provides both berries and blossom in early spring. Grows in all soil types but prefers moist, well-drained soil.

HEIGHT ↕ 10m+ SPREAD ↔ 5m+ FLOWERING ✻ MAY-JUN
POSITION ☼ FULL SUN ☼ PARTIAL SHADE HARDINESS 3 4 5 6 **7**

Common elder

Sambucus nigra

This shrub provides a fond family memory of our grandfather roaming around the fields collecting the flowers for his annual elderflower wine-making. A large bushy shrub, with a slightly shaggy apperance. Grows well in all soil types and can tolerate an exposed site. Prefers the soil moist but well drained.

HEIGHT ↕ 5m+ SPREAD ↔ 2m FLOWERING ✻ JUN
POSITION ☼ FULL SUN ☼ PARTIAL SHADE HARDINESS 3 4 5 **6** 7

Chinese witch hazel

Hamamelis mollis

Really special shrub. Grows in an outward fashion with broad oval leaves dispalying vibrant autumn colour. Most recognisable in late winter when its bare branches display almost paper-like flowers ranging from yellow/orange/red. Grows in moist, well-drained soil, sand, clay or loam. Prefers a sheltered spot

HEIGHT ↕ 3.5m SPREAD ↔ 3.5m FLOWERING ✻ DEC-FEB
POSITION ☼ FULL SUN ☼ PARTIAL SHADE HARDINESS 3 4 **5** 6 7

SUB-CANOPY LAYER

EVERGREEN SHRUBS

English yew
Taxus baccata

An ancient British species, perfect for topiary. Deep green throughout the year, but displaying soft, shaggy, light green spring growth. Grows well in all well-drained soils. Commonly forms the understorey in beech woodlands and has long been planted in churchyards. It density makes it perfect for nesting birds.

HEIGHT ↕ 20m+ SPREAD ↔ 8m FLOWERING ❀ MAR-APR
POSITION ☼◐◐ ANYWHERE! HARDINESS 3 4 5 6 **7**

Oval leaf privet
Ligustrum ovalifolium

You will know privet as a hedging plant, though left to grow naturally, it's a perfect woodland shrub, and as it's dense and bushy it can be used to block off views, providing a dark green backdrop for flowering perennials. Prefers to grow in well-drained soils and can tolerate all soil types.

HEIGHT ↕ 3m SPREAD ↔ 3m FLOWERING ❀ JUL-AUG
POSITION ☼ FULL SUN ◐ PARTIAL SHADE HARDINESS 3 4 **5** 6 7

Box-leaved holly
Ilex crenata

This shrub better resembles box than holly. Slow-growing but can tolerate many diseases that box can't, so a great alternative. Grows well in all but heavy soils and with its compact growing habit is perfect for topiary.

HEIGHT ↕ 3m+ SPREAD ↔ 3m FLOWERING ❀ MAY
POSITION ☼ FULL SUN ◐ PARTIAL SHADE HARDINESS 3 4 5 **6** 7

Cunningham white
Rhododendron 'Roseum Elegans'

Try and find one that has been allowed to grow naturally rather than pruned. This will really capture a leggy woodland understorey feeling. It's a dense, suckering shrub that can cover whole hillsides so be aware of its spreading habit before planting it in your garden. An acid-loving plant that can tolerate nearly neutral.

HEIGHT ↕ 2m+ SPREAD ↔ 2m+ FLOWERING ❀ MAY
POSITION ◐ PARTIAL SHADE HARDINESS 3 4 5 **6** 7

CANOPY LAYER

DECIDUOUS TREES

Ornamental cherry

Prunus 'Accolade'

A real masterpiece: simple, natural bark, ovate leaf and a stunning soft-pink display of blossom in spring. Great tree for small gardens. Tolerates all moist, well-drained soils. Grows in a spreading, branching habit.

HEIGHT ↕ 8m SPREAD ↔ 8m FLOWERING ❋ APR-MAY
POSITION ☼ FULL SUN HARDINESS 3 4 5 6 7

Snow mespilus / Juneberry

Amelanchier lamarckii

A stunning tree that is widely used, but you can see why. Its stems alone provide sculpture in the garden, it displays orange-red leaves in the autumn, blossoms in spring, and produces a tasty edible berry in summer. Grows well in clay, sand and loam soils that are moist and well-drained.

HEIGHT ↕ 10m+ SPREAD ↔ 8m+ FLOWERING ❋ MAR-APR
POSITION ☼ FULL SUN ☼ PARTIAL SHADE HARDINESS 3 4 5 6 7

Downy birch

Betula pubescens

A great alternative to Betula pendula *as its bark is a more subtle silver-white , it tolerates damper conditions and can grow at higher altitudes. It displays catkins in spring (lambs' tails) and its dappled canopy is great for letting light through to the understorey. Can tolerate exposure to wind and all soil types*

HEIGHT ↕ 12m+ SPREAD ↔ 5m+ FLOWERING ❋ APR-MAY
PPOSITION ☼ FULL SUN ☼ PARTIAL SHADE HARDINESS 3 4 5 6 7

Field maple

Acer campestre

Stunning tree both single- and multi-stemmed. Young bark has a rough grain and the display of vivid gold in autumn is beautiful. Has a bushy, compact growing habit. Thrives in all soils provided they are moist and well drained.

HEIGHT ↕ 12m+ SPREAD ↔ 5m+ FLOWERING ❋ APR-MAY
POSITION ☼ FULL SUN ☼ PARTIAL SHADE HARDINESS 3 4 5 6 7

TREE + SHRUB SUITABILITY

Choosing the right trees and shrubs for your garden is vital to the development of the woodland. This table provides a selection of woodland trees and shrubs and the conditions they thrive in.

TREE SPECIES	Wet/moist	Heavy	Neutral/alkaline	Acid	Light/dry	Exposed	Shady
Ash Fraxinus excelsior	×	×	×		×	×	
Aspen Populus tremula		×	×	×	×	×	
Black Poplar Populus nigra	×	×	×				
Common alder Alnus glutinosa	×		×				
Crab apple Malus sylvestris		×		×	×		
Downy birch Betula pubescens	×	×	×	×	×	×	
Field maple Acer campestre		×			×	×	
Goat willow Salix caprea	×		×			×	
Larch Larix decidua			×	×	×	×	
Large-leaved lime Tilia platyphyllos		×	×				×
Oak Quercus robur	×	×	×	×			×
Pine Pinus aucuparia			×	×	×	×	
Rowan Sorbus acuparia				×	×	×	
Sessile oak Quercus petraea			×	×	×		×
Small-leaved lime Tilia cordata		×	×	×	×		×
Silver birch Betula pendula	×	×	×	×	×		
Sweet chestnut Castanea sativa					×		
Wild cherry Prunus avium		×	×			×	
SHRUB SPECIES							
Alder buckthorn Frangula alnus			×		×		
Bay willow Salix pentandra	×		×				
Blackthorn Prunus spinosa	×	×	×		×	×	
Dog rose Rosa canina		×	×		×	×	
Dogwood Cornus sanguinea		×	×		×	×	
Elder Sambucus nigra		×	×		×		
Field rose Rosa arvensis		×	×				
Hawthorn Crataegus monogyna	×	×	×	×	×	×	
Hazel Corylus avellana	×				×	×	
Holly Ilex aquifolium			×	×	×	×	
Privet Ligustrum ovalifolium		×	×		×	×	
Purging buckthorn Rhamnus cathartica		×	×			×	
Spindle Euonymus europaea		×	×		×		

DESIGNING A WOODLAND

This series of sketches outlines the process you should undertake when designing a woodland. We always break it down into these four steps. It makes the process more manageable and provides a clearer focus on the individual elements and how they work together. This is a section of a larger woodland design, but these same stages can be used in a smaller setting, too.

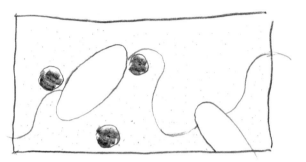

1: GLADES + PATHS

Draw out areas for open glades. These will allow light to filter through to the woodland floor, creating perfect conditions for field layer planting, helping to enhance the biodiversity by creating varying habitats.

We have positioned the glades so that they are surrounded by trees and shrubs, heightening the sense of enclosure whilst providing vital breathing spaces along the way.

2: MAJOR TREES

Position the larger trees first as they can be slower-growing, causing them to become shaded by faster-growing species. These larger trees can be planted at the same time as the whole woodland but make sure you allow them more surrounding space to grow into.

Pick out key spots along your route. Positioning major trees close to glades will allow the branches room to stretch out over time.

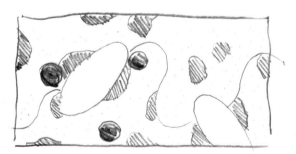

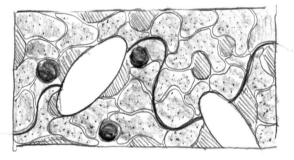

3: SHRUBS

Introducing shrubs within the woodland creates infill, whilst planting them on the perimeter will create a graded edge, helping to shelter the trees and encourage wildlife.

Shrubs provide animals and birds with cover, habitats and nesting sites.

4: TREES

Introduce trees within an informal layout. Varied spacing and planting in small groups of the same species will help to reduce competition as the woodland grows. Groups should contain between 20–60 trees.

Space your trees at a minimum of 3×3m, creating a density of 1,100 trees per hectare. This will provide you with an accessible community woodland.

TEST CONDITIONS

If you are in any doubt about the soil conditions you should dig soil pits of up to 1m in depth at different points within your garden. If constraints such as compacted soil, very heavy clay soil or plough pan are present they could prove detrimental to your woodland development.

STUDY YOUR SURROUNDINGS

Studying the surrounding landscape can help determine the scale and type of woodland appropriate for your land. Larger woodland may fit best with open arable land whereas individual fields and more secluded surroundings may suit a smaller woodland. This can also help you to discover what trees and shrubs do best in your area and how they work best together.

PICK A GOOD TIME OF YEAR TO PLANT

Trees and shrubs should be planted between November and the end of March, before they start coming into bud.

TYPES OF PLANT STOCK

BARE-ROOT TRANSPLANTS are the cheapest, easiest to plant and most widely available stock. However, they will need to be handled with care and are prone to dying out. It's best to plant these straight away but they can be stored in specially made bags for up to 4 weeks in a cool, shaded spot.

CELL-GROWN plants have been grown in small plastic cells so come with soil around them and can

be stored for longer then bare-root. These will be more expensive than bare-root and will need more care when planting as frost can force the cells out of the ground.

WHIPS, FEATHERED WHIPS + STANDARDS are generally larger trees, best for a more instant effect. These again will be more expensive and have a much higher rate of loss. The size of these trees and shrubs will make them harder to transport and plant.

SETTS are cuttings of species such as willow and poplar and can be planted directly into the ground, making the process a lot quicker and easier. Setts will require a wet spring otherwise many may die.

CONTAINER-GROWN larger trees and shrubs have a honeycomb plastic sleeve surrounding the entire root system, allowing air pruning of the roots. This technique creates a more fibrous root system.

WOODLAND PROTECTION + MAINTENANCE

TREE PROTECTION

There are many different types of tree protection, including spiral guards, sleeves and mesh barriers (as shown below), but all provide a physical boundary between the young tree and wildlife. If you have planted the trees very young this will help to locate them.

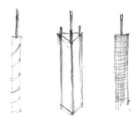

ENCOURAGING BIRDS OF PREY

A great way to encourage birds of prey into the woodland is to provide them with tall posts to hunt from. It's a great natural way to help with pest control.

WEED PREVENTION

Using wood or bark chip at the base of the tree smothers weeds and prevents them from germinating. It's a great alternative to matting as it's organic, easy to use and suits more environmentally sensitive sites.

REPLACING DEAD TREES

Assess the trees in August after they have had a chance to come into leaf. You can replace with the same species, though it can be a good idea to look if there is a species doing noticably better and replace with that, keeping in mind the overall aim of the woodland.

CONSTRUCTING DECKING

Timber is a beautiful material to use. Not only is it resilient and adaptable, it also provides a tactile experience.

Timber is relatively easy to work with, is accessible, and brings a warmth and a natural quality to any space.

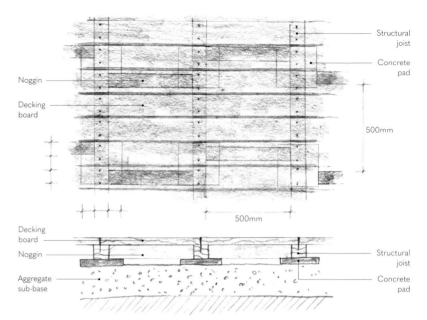

Structural joist

Concrete pad

Noggin

Decking board

500mm

500mm

Decking board

Noggin

Aggregate sub-base

Structural joist

Concrete pad

1: FOUNDATIONS

Dig out the area where the deck will sit to approximately 100mm. This will vary due to the stability of your soil. Fill the dug out with an aggregate sub-base and compact it using a wacker plate. Make the surface as level as possible.

Place the concrete slabs onto a pad of mortar. At this stage it is crucial that the tops of the pads are all the correct level as this is what the joists sit on. Packers can be used beneath the joist if needed.

2: FRAMEWORK

Construct the outer frame first and use structural joists to span the distance against the proposed direction of the decking boards. Different-sized joists can achieve different heights but they should be no thinner than 50mm. Space them approximately 500mm apart.

To strengthen the joist attach noggins in between and alternate their spacing so you can screw through the joist into the end of the noggin. Space these approximately 500mm apart.

At each join use two external grade 150mm screws. Make sure the framework stays level and square. The best way to check this is to measure its diagonals:

diagonal length = side length × square root of 2 [approx. 1.41]

3: DECKING

Loose lay the decking boards out against the direction of the joist and determine the spacing. Between 2–5mm is advised as you need to take swelling into account.

Secure the boards to the joist with decking screws. The size needed will vary but approximately 65mm is fine. Use two screws per board to each and every joist to avoid cupping. Position the screws about 15mm in from the edge of each board to avoid splitting.

FOUNDATION TYPES FOR DECKING

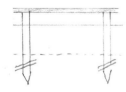

Wooden posts are rammed into the ground until firm.

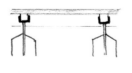

A steel component is set into a concrete foundation on which the deck sits.

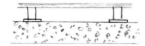

Paving slabs sit on top of an aggregate sub-base. This elevates the posts off the ground.

The use of adjustable feet makes it possible to level up the deck on sloping ground.

"... We parked the Landrover in a remote part of the forest and set up camp. Looking back through the pines as the sunlight warmed their bark, we realised it wasn't to do with the gear, the boards, the trip – it was about being alone in the wild ..."

GRASSLAND

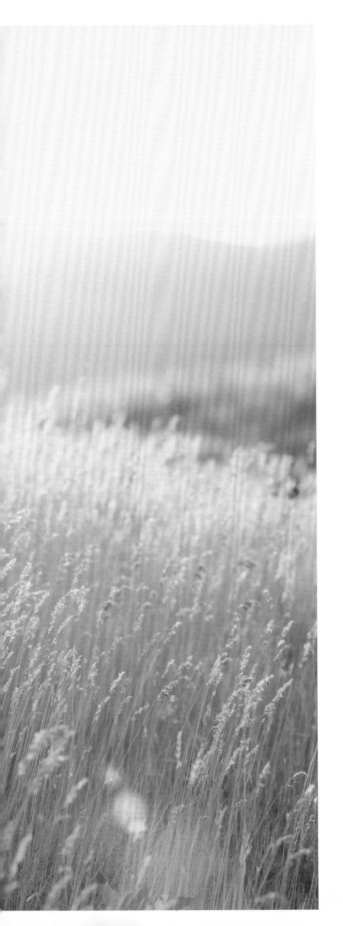

"When we were young Dad used to let us cut the hay meadow on a Massey Ferguson tractor known as Noddy. It was a great experience and we learned a lot about the actual process of making hay while the sun shines."

Grasslands are complex networks of plants. They are comprised of large drifts of grasses interspersed with seasonal perennials such as Echinacea, Digitalis and Sanguisorba that all fuse together to create some of the most beautiful and effective plant combinations. We feel these plant communities exemplify nature's complexity, depth and balance, and they have inspired us to incorporate more naturalistic planting within many of our designs.

To us plants are the living fabric in any garden, with the ability to dictate the atmosphere within the simplest of designs. When we create our planting schemes we always look at them like paintings. Colours, brushstrokes and individual details are fundamental to the process.

Grasslands vary widely across the world. Their vegetation can differ in height quite dramatically, from a foot or so on the chalk grasslands of southern England to five foot in the tall grass prairies of Northern America.

TEMPERATE GRASSLANDS

Temperate grasslands are enormous areas of prairie, savanna and steppe characterised by moderate temperatures, moderate rainfall and few trees.

These temperate grasslands appear across the world. In many places the grasslands cannot be considered true grassland due to human influences on the land such as farming.

PRAIRIE

STEPPE

SAVANNA

PLAINS OF NORTH AMERICA

The Great Plains are an expanse of flat land situated west of the Mississippi River tallgrass prairie states and east of the Rocky Mountains. The Great Plains have a wide range of weather over the year, from very cold and harsh winters to hot and humid summers, making the plants that grow there very hardy.

The largest central mixed prairie is dominated by several species of grasses. Stipa, Agropyron, Bouteloua and Koeleria. The North is dominated by Festuca and Helictotrichon, West by Bouteloua gracilis and Buchloe dactyloides and the East the bluestem grasses Andropogon gerardii and A. scoparium.

PAMPAS OF SOUTH AMERCA

The Pampas are fertile lowlands connecting Argentina, Uruguay and Brazil. The climate ranges from cool to very warm and humid and rainfall is more or less evenly distributed across the year, creating a rich area of prairies.

Among many grasses the Stipa is the most diverse, with other species such as Paspalum and Andropogon.

STEPPES OF EURASIA

This is the vast steppe eco-region of temperate grasslands, savannas, prairie and shrublands biome. It extends thousands of miles from Eastern Europe almost to the Pacific ocean, bound on the north by the forests of Russia and Siberia. The climate varies greatly across the steppes.

Varied species of Stipa dominate the majority of the flora, mixed in areas with other dominant species such as Festuca and Agropyron.

SAHEL + VELDT OF AFRICA

The Sahel and Veldt are wide, open, rural landscapes that make up the central band across the east to west and south into the middle of South Africa.

The Sahel bridges the continent, forming the largest area of tropical grassland containing common grasses such as Aristida, Cenchrus, and Schoenefeldia. The East can contain grasses such as Hyparrhenia and Pennisetum due to the wetter conditions and grassses such as Aristida and Chrysopogon in the drier areas. The Veld regions support an enormous variety of natural vegetation with the dominant species of red grass growing in well-drained, fertile areas.

DOWNLANDS OF AUSTRALIA

In Northern Australia most of the region is covered in tropical and subtropical savanna, creating vast plains of tall dense grass with few pockets of woodland.

Grasses such as Plectrachne triodia, Heteropogon, Sorghum and Astrebla thrive here.

BRITISH MEADOWS

Like prairies, Britian's meadows differ according to geological composition, soil type and management.

The oldest, most diverse meadows were once found in forest clearings. This diversity was due to never being ploughed, preserving the land with all its hollows and slopes intact, providing different habitats for plants that favoured wet or dry soil conditions.

In Britain there are three distinct types of meadow, each defined by the soil conditions on which it grows.

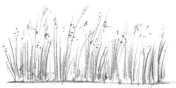

ACID GRASSLAND

Acid grasslands typically occur on nutrient-poor, free-draining soil with a pH of 4–5.5. These soils overlie rocks such as sandstone or igneous rock, and deposits of sand and gravel.

These meadows contain grasses, rushes and sedges but tend to have fewer flowers compared to neutral or calcareous grassland. They are characterised by grassy, mossy vegetation.

NEUTRAL GRASSLAND

Neutral grasslands are flower-rich meadows located on fertile pastoral land. These are areas of managed grassland, unimproved by fertilisers, that are cut for hay in late June/ early July after the display of summer flowers.

These meadows occur on soil that is neither strongly acid nor alkaline.

CALCAREOUS GRASSLAND

Calcareous grasslands develop on shallow, basic soils rich in lime and with poor nutritional levels. They mainly occur in the warmer and drier south and east of the UK, typically on dry valley slopes.

Upland calcareous grasslands are found on open windswept hillsides, and in some cases in the UK support rare species that are more commonly found in the Alps. Vegetation is typically short and hardy.

Heath bedstraw
Galium saxatile

Sheep's fescue
Festuca ovina

Common bent
Agrostis capillaris

Sheep's sorrel
Rumex acetosella

Wavy hair grass
Deschampsia flexuosa

Pill sedge
Carex pilulifera

Tormentil
Potentialla erecta

Quaking grass
Briza media

Sweet vernal grass
Anthoxanthum odoratum

Crested dog's tail
Cynosurus cristatus

Red fescue
Festuca rubra

Devil's bit scabious
Succisa pratensis

Pepper saxifrage
Silaum silaus

Green-winged orchid
Anacamptis morio

Snakeshead fritillary
Fritillaria meleagris

Adder's tongue fern
Ophioglossum vulgatum

In damper areas:

Cuckooflower
Cardamine pratensis

Ragged robin
Lychnis flos-cuculi

Yellow iris
Iris pseudacorus

Salad burnet
Sanguisorba minor

Bird's foot refoil
Lotus corniculatus

Upright brome
Bromus madritensis

Blue moor grass
Sesleria caerulea

Common rock rose
Helianthemum nummularium

Spring gentian
Gentiana verna

Alpine forget-me-not
Myosotis alpestris

Mountain avens
Dryas octopetala

Calcareous grasslands are filled with rich aromas of herbs such as:

Thyme
Thymus

Marjoram
Origanum majorana

Wild basil
Calamintha acinos

ELEMENT
REPETITION

Within grasslands finding twenty-five or more species per square metre is not unusual. Repetition of plant varieties is unavoidable: when you look closely at a grassland planting scheme, it is apparent that species are freely repeated throughout.

Often it's the emergent plants that catch your eye first and the repetition of these bold architectural forms sets the character and tone of the scheme.

Foxglove Digitalis purpurea growing out of lower vegetation in mid-summer. This emergent plant will catch your eye, leading it around the planting scheme

Repetition of grasses is also very important – they interweave between the individual plant groups, fusing the scheme together whilst providing movement and subtle details.

A large drift of Stipa tenuissima. Planting grasses en masse creates a dramatic effect, especially when the wind blows through them

PRINCIPLE
BALANCE

Wild plant communities are the result of a natural equilibrium achieved over many cycles of growth. There is something very calming about the sight of a flowering meadow that has evolved in this way.

In a naturalistic planting scheme the aim is to achieve a perfect balance between form, height, colour and texture.

It is fundamental when creating a planting scheme to look at the key plants you will be using, as these can determine the atmosphere within your garden. The natural planting scheme above features a predominantly green backdrop, with upon that a sizeable proportion of white and yellow. The smaller yellow flower has been balanced by a larger white one. Finally, unlike the well-defined pockets of Coreopsis palmata and Queen Anne's lace and white planting, pale pink Echinacea sanguinea is scattered throughout to blur the boundaries.

ELEMENT
SHAPE

Grasslands are always moving and adapting. Plants tend to grow in communities, establishing themselves in conditions that best suit their requirements. These plant groupings help to shape the overall scheme, creating pockets and drifts that draw the eye through the planting.

Grasslands are predominantly flat, any shape within them created by the contrasting colours and forms of the plants. When you get pockets of the same species repeated across a grassland, they form an intricate, almost fluid patchwork.

This meadow demonstrates the way the subtle differences between the plants' colour and texture contribute to the overall effect. We've highlighted these shapes on the photo with a faint white line

Pockets of **Poppies**
Papaver rhoeas impose
shape within the field.
Their contrasting flower
shape and bold colour
create a very distinctive
pattern

The intricate shape
and detail of the
Spear thistle
Cirsium vulgare
in flower

ELEMENT
TEXTURE

Each plant species provides its own individual texture, but when we look at a garden this isn't something we consciously consider. We do, however, recognise it subconsciously. Textures hold and reflect light differently, reflecting colours or creating shadows, and these added details help to create depth and interest amongst the planting.

The foliage of
the **Goldenrod**
Solidago gigantea
contrasting with
the grasses' more
delicate stems

Wintertime strips the colour from a garden, making the texture of plants more evident. The raw form of the seedhead and the bare structure of the plant are displayed, bringing an understated new beauty to the planting beds.

Textures can also come from foliage. These can be used to create a subtle connection or an obvious contrast, allowing you to pick out the individual plant from within the scheme. When the texture of two species is similar it knits them into a complementary grouping that is softer on the eye.

Black-eyed Susan
Rudbeckia hirta
covered with frost
in winter

INSPIRATION

This area of meadow really inspired us. Its muted colour scheme provided a sense of harmony. A subtle path drifted through the waist-high meadow; its direction was obscured by the long grasses, giving it an endless feeling.

We wanted to emphasise the curved endless lines within this to create a network of narrow sympathetic paths leading to a functional lawn. A few considered trees provide scale, adding a subtle framework to the garden.

ISLANDS OF PLANTING

GENTLE
LANDFORM

OPEN
LAWN

MOWN GRASS PATHS

Isolating individual colours from a grassland habitat can be a great way of working out a scheme for your planting. This photo shows a section of prairie with a higher density of perennials to grasses, providing a wider colour spectrum.

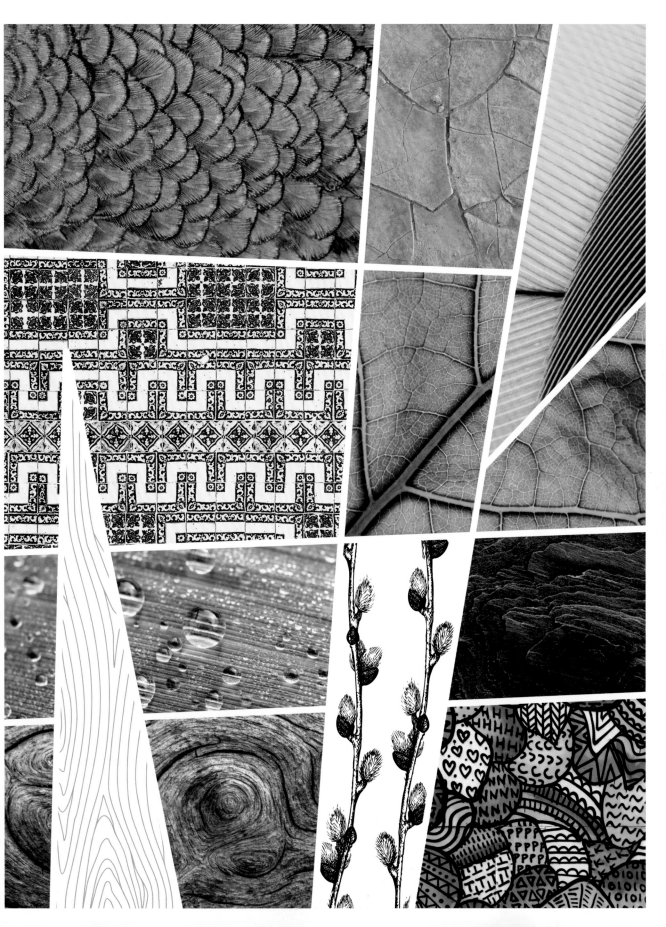

DESIGN CONCEPTS

PLANTING BED DESIGN

Planting beds don't just need to run along the perimter of your garden, but instead become the heart of the design. Shape, size and direction can all play an important part in determining a specific character. Planting beds can be soft and curved, encouraging a more informal journey, or more controlled, constraining you to a set route.

It's great to get inspiration from things outside the gardening world. When creating planting bed shapes we look at fabrics and colour within fashion, architectural strucure, and shapes and patterns found in nature.

These planting beds have been inspired by the layout of city streets. This arrangement creates engaging narrow pathways that vary in size and direction.

A gridded area opens up many possibilities for planting bed arrangements.

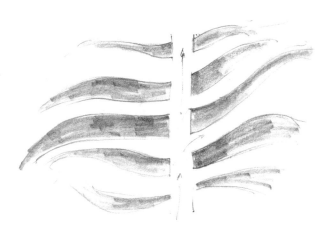

Drifts of planting contrast with a straight path. The relationship between the two opposing directions creates interest and drama.

The straight lines within this design have been disjointed by asymmetical circles. This leaves open various spaces at different points in the garden to be used for seating or other features.

Teardrop-shaped beds inspire free-flowing movement through the space.

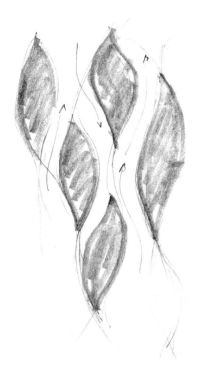

The line of planting can be set back from the path, creating space for seating off the walkway.

Inspired by the repetitive pattern created by a school of fish. These shapes convey an instant feeling of flow and movement.

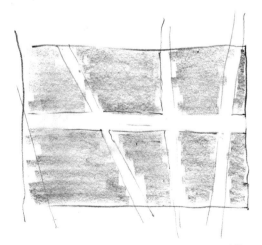

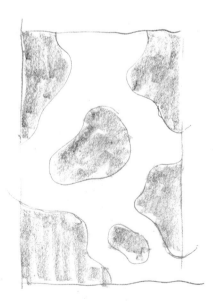

Diagonal paths intersect the central path at different stages, splitting the space into individual areas and adding depth to the design.

Having one central bed creates two routes through the garden. On the ground you would see only planting, with the path diverging and forcing you to choose your next direction.

PLANTING BED DESIGN

A modular honeycomb layout makes it easy to create structure within your garden.

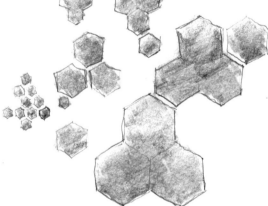

Cell-shaped beds with routes through scattered planting – organic and flexible.

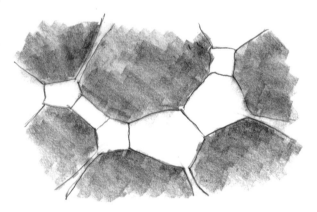

Varied honeycomb shapes share the same character but differ in size. This detail brings harmony and unity to the design.

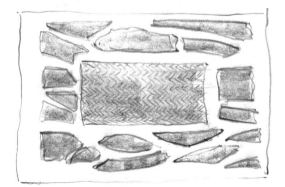

A central open space can be introduced, providing breathing space from the surrounding planting – and a great viewpoint.

Cell-like structures form the planting beds. It's easy to remove these to form open space or to include them around existing features.

The leaf form is always inspiring. Recreating the outlines of the mid-rib and veins gives routes and connectivity to your space. This leaves the lamina of the leaf to function as planting or lawn.

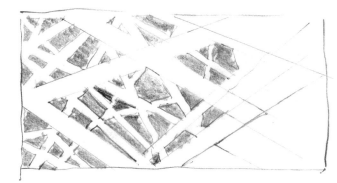

Leaf veins have inspired these interconnecting pathways, leaving large, open areas for planting.

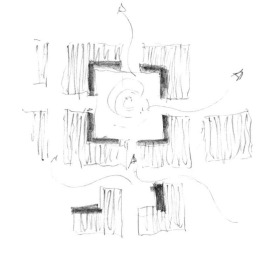

A geometric layout. Four smaller squares have been cut into to form one large open square. It keeps the same rhythm and allows for a seating space or a point of interest. Low box hedging can be used to define the shapes within the design.

Inspired by a traditional carpentry dovetail joint on a piece of furniture, this shape gives structure and interest to a simple linear planting bed.

A different perspective reveals how the dovetail-inspired hedging both opens up and restricts views into the planting beds.

A PRAIRIE GARDEN

INITIAL DESIGN PLAN

Design separate 'rooms' that are connected through planting, giving the character of a flat expanse of grassland

Provide a single route through the garden that is opposed by structural forms, defining the rooms

Position a seating space within the middle section, surrounded by planting

Create a natural backdrop using shrubs and trees

HOUSE

CONCEPT DEVELOPMENT

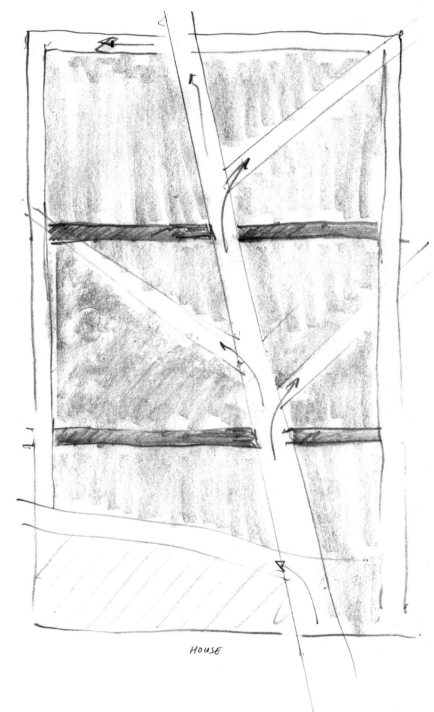

HOUSE

The idea is that this could be a section within a larger garden. The paths could lead out into different paths of a larger design

To separate the two beds created either side of the central path, we have introduced secondary paths. Their direction is inspired by a branching tree

When walking from the house into the garden the branching paths encourage you to stray from the central path as their angle is more gentle and inviting.

When returning to the house the acute angle causes the paths to become hidden from view, providing a more isolated route through the planting

Low topiary hedges create structured but natural divisions

CONCEPT DEVELOPMENT

We decided to confine the seating to the middle area. It provides a more immersive space under the canopy of the adjacent tree

The two open spaces have a great sense of connection and this design allows the garden to be used more practically

To create more of a prairie feeling, planting beds cover two-thirds of the garden

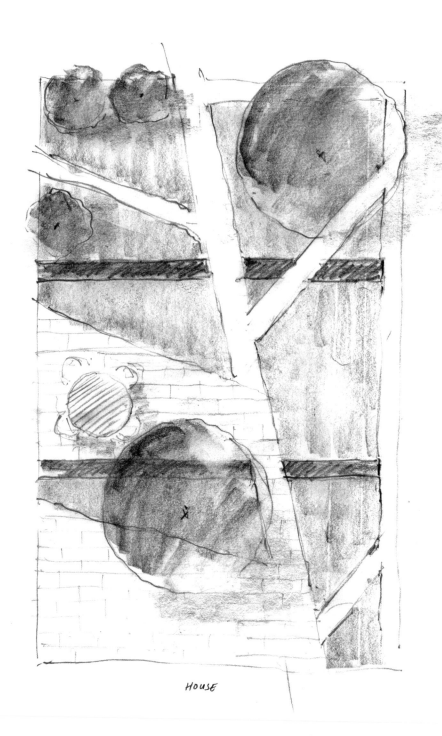

HOUSE

FINAL DESIGN

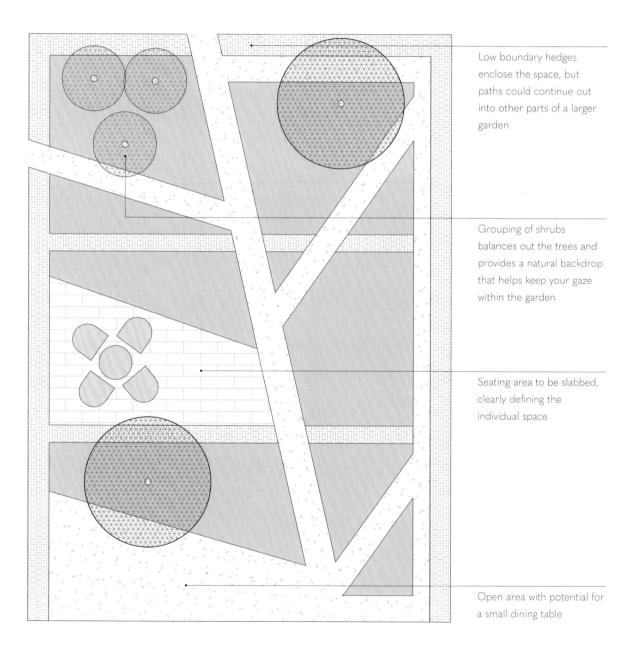

Low boundary hedges
enclose the space, but
paths could continue out
into other parts of a larger
garden

Grouping of shrubs
balances out the trees and
provides a natural backdrop
that helps keep your gaze
within the garden

Seating area to be slabbed,
clearly defining the
individual space

Open area with potential for
a small dining table

FINAL DESIGN VISUALS

Strong repeated box hedging forms a natural framework for the prairie planting within. The two small multi-stemmed trees provide balance and vertical interest. The space nestled beween the two hedges provides the perfect sheltered seating area.

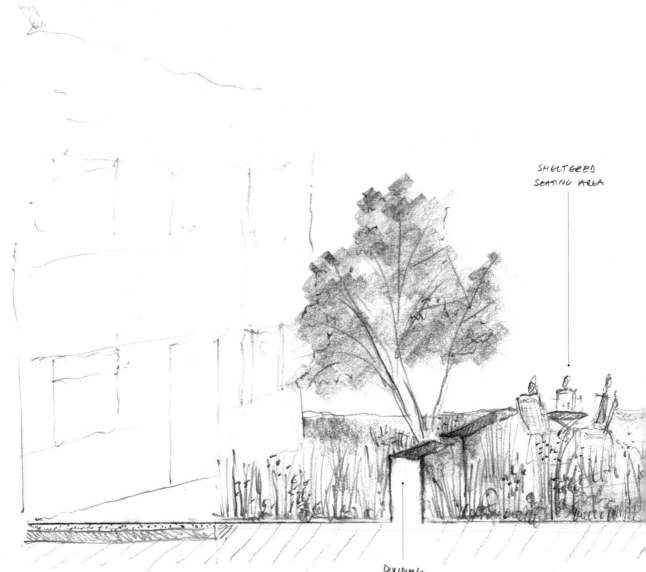

SHELTERED
SEATING AREA

DIVIDING
HEDGING

While still keeping the space open, two multi-stemmed *Amelanchier* trees add height to the garden. Without these it would feel flat and lack any vertical interest.

SHRUB
LAYER

PRAIRIE
PLANTING

MULTI-STEM TREES /
DAPPLED CANOPY

GRASSLAND PLANTING

We have a fondness for grasses, which we feel stems from childhood memories of running through the hay meadow at home. When designing a planting scheme we always use a select palette of grasses, carefully chosen to enhance the atmosphere of the space.

We tend to choose grasses that make a less obvious impression, diffusing their forms and colour through the planting rather than dominating it. This hazy characteristic is intriguing. We have never been fans of the obvious. A garden needs to be multi-layered, leading you on to discover its finer details.

Grasses display their warm-coloured framework during the winter. The low light accentuates this golden tone, which is complemented by the earthy hues of other overwintering plants.

Grasses inject life into a garden. The way they offset the forms and colours of neighbouring plants has the ability to alter the mood of a border dramatically. Vertical-spired plants such as the Digitalis ferruginea echo the upright form of grasses, creating a harmonious association.

Umbellifers are another group of plants that complement grasses. Their flat-topped umbels provide horizontal interest, which contrasts well with grasses' more upright habit.

MEADOW EFFECT
PLANTING MIX

This mix provides the individual species that will create a sympathetic meadow grassland within your garden.

PRIMARY SPECIES <60%

↑ Meadow foxtail
Alopecurus pratensis

Slender creeping red fescue
Festuca rubra ssp. litoralis

Meadow fescue
Festuca pratensis

Crested dog's tail
Cynosurus cristatus

Rough-stalked meadow grass
Poa trivialis

Tufted hair grass
Deschampsia cespitosa

Golden oat grass
Trisetum flavescens

Yorkshire fog
Holcus lanatus

Smaller cat's tail
Phleum bertolonii

Yellow rattle
Rhinanthus minor

SECONDARY SPECIES <30%

↑ Ribwort plantain
Plantago lanceolata

Common knapweed
Centaurea nigra

Lady's bedstraw
Galium verum

Meadow buttercup
Ranunculus acris

Creeping buttercup
Ranunculus repens

Meadowsweet
Filipendula ulmaria

Common sorrel
Rumex acetosa

TERTIARY SPECIES <10%

↑ Yarrow
Achillea millefolium

Agrimony
Agrimonia eupatoria

Creeping bent
Agrostis stolonifera

Self-heal
Prunella vulgaris

Meadow vetchling
Lathyris pratensis

Autumn hawkbit
Leontodon autumnalis

Quaking grass
Briza media

Dandelion
Taraxacum officinale

Red clover
Trifolium pratense

White clover
Trifolium repens

MEADOW EFFECT

PERENNIALS

Yarrow
Achillea millefolium

Attracting many beneficial insects, this plant is perfect for the middle layer of a planting bed. Flattened clusters of small daisy-like flowerheads sit above aromatic fern-like leaves, creating a lovely detail against grasses.

HEIGHT ↕ 0.9m SPREAD ↔ 0.3m FLOWERING ❋ MAY-AUG
POSITION ☼ FULL SUN HARDINESS 3 4 5 6 **7**

Drumstick allium
Allium sphaerocephalon

These oval flowerheads start off green, turning pink then deep red. We love using this allium to pop up amongst planting, losing its nondescript foliage and revealing a bold and unexpected form.

HEIGHT ↕ 0.9m SPREAD ↔ 0.08m FLOWERING ❋ JUL-AUG
POSITION ☼ FULL SUN HARDINESS 3 4 5 **6** 7

Coneflower
Echinacea purpurea 'White Swan'

A shaggy, white daisy flower which looks just as distinguished during the winter. Its sepia tones and seedheads are great against grasses.

HEIGHT ↕ 0.7m SPREAD ↔ 0.45m FLOWERING ❋ JUN-SEP
POSITION ☼ FULL SUN HARDINESS 3 4 5 6 **7**

White heath aster
Aster 'Monte Cassino'

A mist of delicate white daisy-shaped flowerheads make this a great filler plant. Its sympathetic blanket effect brings unity and a sense of harmony within a scheme.

HEIGHT ↕ 1m SPREAD ↔ 0.5m FLOWERING ❋ AUG-OCT
POSITION ☼ FULL SUN ◐ PARTIAL SHADE HARDINESS 3 4 5 6 **7**

3 hardy in coastal and relatively mild parts of the UK [-5 to 1°C]
4 hardy through most of the UK [-10 to -5°C]
5 hardy in most places throughout the UK, even in severe winters [-15 to -10°C]
6 hardy in all of UK and northern Europe [-20 to -15°C]
7 hardy in the severest European continental climates [-20°C and lower]

Meadowsweet
Filipendula ulmaria

Growing in damper conditions, meadowsweet produces creamy-white flowers on frothy plumes, providing a soft but striking detail amongst your planting scheme.

HEIGHT ↕ 0.9m SPREAD ↔ 0.3m   FLOWERING ❋ JUN–AUG
POSITION ☼ FULL SUN ☽ PARTIAL SHADE   HARDINESS ③ ④ ⑤ ❻ ⑦

Bee balm / Bergamot
Monarda 'Croftway Pink'

A naturalising plant with light pink flowerheads, perfect for the middle of a planting scheme. They will produce long periods of flowering, looking great in large drifts.

HEIGHT ↕ 0.9m SPREAD ↔ 0.45m   FLOWERING ❋ JUL–SEP
POSITION ☼ FULL SUN ☽ PARTIAL SHADE   HARDINESS ③ ❹ ⑤ ⑥ ⑦

Sage-leaf mullein
Phlomis tuberosa 'Amazone'

A dramatic presence, its strong vertical form reveals lilac beads on tiered stems. In winter the seedheads provide a distinctive silhouette amongst grasses. A very robust and versatile perennial that will provide continued interest throughout the year.

HEIGHT ↕ 1.2m SPREAD ↔ 0.9m   FLOWERING ❋ JUL–AUG
POSITION ☼ FULL SUN   HARDINESS ③ ❹ ⑤ ❄▲ ⑥ ⑦

Cow parsley
Anthriscus sylvestris

Delicate umbels of tiny white flowers are perfect for naturalising a planting scheme. We see it everywhere in Wales, especially down the small lane that leads back to our parents' house.

HEIGHT ↕ 0.1m SPREAD ↔ 0.3m   FLOWERING ❋ MAY–JUL
POSITION ☼ FULL SUN ☽ PARTIAL SHADE   HARDINESS ③ ④ ⑤ ❻ ⑦

MEADOW EFFECT

GRASSES

Wavy hair grass
Deschampsia flexuosa

Narrow and finely textured, this clump-forming perennial grass adds an airy atmosphere to any planting scheme, moving in the lightest of breezes. A great plant for dapped shade.

HEIGHT ↕ 0.6m SPREAD ↔ 0.3m FLOWERING APR–MAY
POSITION PARTIAL SHADE SHADE HARDINESS 3 4 5 6 7

Silky spike melic
Melica ciliata

An evergreen clump-forming grass providing an abundance of creamy blooms in early autumn. Planted en masse it can thread through a formal or informal planting scheme.

HEIGHT ↕ 1m SPREAD ↔ 0.5m FLOWERING MAY–JUN
POSITION FULL SUN PARTIAL SHADE HARDINESS 3 4 5 6 7

Quaking grass
Briza media

Large quaking seedheads erupt above an evergreen clump of foliage. We almost always use this in a shady scheme, it creates a fine hazy texture.

HEIGHT ↕ 0.9m SPREAD ↔ 0.3m FLOWERING MAY–AUG
POSITION FULL SUN HARDINESS 3 4 5 6 7

Rough feather grass
Stipa calamagrostis

A really handsome, bushy deciduous grass with narrow arching leaves and a mass of large feathery panicles in summer. Looks stunning in winter with its strong form and sepia tone. Grows best in medium to light, well-drained soil.

HEIGHT ↕ 1m SPREAD ↔ 1.2m FLOWERING JUN–SEP
POSITION FULL SUN HARDINESS 3 4 5 6 7

Tufted hair grass

Deschampsia cespitosa

A bushy evergreen grass formed of tough dark leaves, producing a beautiful haze of feathery flowers in summer. An easy plant to grow as it can tolerate most soils, from dry to moist.

HEIGHT ↕ 1.5m SPREAD ↔ 1m FLOWERING ✿ JUN-AUG
POSITION ☀ FULL SUN ⛅ PARTIAL SHADE HARDINESS [3] [4] [5] **[6]** [7]

Chinese fountain grass

Pennisetum alopecuroides

Narrow green foliage and bottle-brush flowers turning silvery-pink to purple throughout the year, maturing to shades of brown. The foamy flowerhead adds a soft naturalistic touch to any planting scheme.

HEIGHT ↕ 1.25m SPREAD ↔ 0.6m FLOWERING ✿ JUN-AUG
POSITION ☀ FULL SUN HARDINESS [3] [4] [5] [6] **[7]**

Switch grass

Panicum virgatum

Pendant clusters of metal-grey spikelets provide airy movement, whilst the vertical form adds structure and interest amongst looser planting.

HEIGHT ↕ 1.2m SPREAD ↔ 0.6m FLOWERING ✿ AUG-OCT
POSITION ☀ FULL SUN ⛅ PARTIAL SHADE HARDINESS [3] [4] [5] [6] **[7]**

Chinese silver grass

Miscanthus sinensis 'Gracillimus'

A compact clump of narrow green foliage with tall, lacy, feathered flowers, later turning bronze. It provides strong form and structure amongst planting and holds its form throughout the year. Tolerates most soil conditions.

HEIGHT ↕ 1.5m SPREAD ↔ 0.45m FLOWERING ✿ JUN-SEP
POSITION ☀ FULL SUN HARDINESS [3] [4] [5] [6] **[7]**

PRAIRIE EFFECT

PERENNIALS

Giant blue hyssop
Agastache foeniculum

Perfect for adding vertical accents to your planting scheme. A mass of slender, soft purple spikes held in dark bracts provide long-lasting displays above aromatic foliage. A great plant to add repetition to your planting bed.

HEIGHT ↕ 1m SPREAD ↔ 0.4m FLOWERING ❋ JUL–OCT
POSITION ☼ FULL SUN HARDINESS 3 4 5 **6** 7

Michaelmas daisy
Aster frikartii 'Mönch'

Topped with masses of lavender-blue daisy flowers this aster is normally the first to flower in July/August. Looks incredible in pockets and combines beautifully with grasses, working well at the front and in the middle of borders.

HEIGHT ↕ 0.9m SPREAD ↔ 0.4m FLOWERING ❋ JUL–SEP
POSITION ☼ FULL SUN HARDINESS 3 4 5 6 **7**

Great burnet
Sanguisorba officinalis 'Red Thunder'

Deep-ruby button flowers stand tall on wiry stems with luscious toothed foliage forming attractive ground cover. Their distinctive silhouette offers a dramatic touch to your planting scheme.

HEIGHT ↕ 1.2m SPREAD ↔ 0.6m FLOWERING ❋ JUN–SEP
POSITION ☼ FULL SUN ☼ PARTIAL SHADE HARDINESS 3 4 5 6 **7**

Sneezeweed
Helenium 'Moerheim Beauty'

Dark brown-centred, coppery-red flowerheads produce a powerful display in the summer. This looks great with grasses and earthy yellow-toned plants. The varied colours on their leaves provide an interesting detail.

HEIGHT ↕ 1.25m SPREAD ↔ 0.6m FLOWERING ❋ JUN–AUG
POSITION ☼ FULL SUN HARDINESS 3 4 5 6 **7**

PRAIRIE EFFECT

PERENNIALS

Red bistort
Persicaria amplexicaulis 'Firetail'

Dark green arrow-shaped foliage surrounds slender, dark crimson spikes up to 15cm long. It provides a naturalistic touch to a planting scheme and although vigorous is non-invasive. A real favourite of ours.

HEIGHT ↕ 1.2m SPREAD ↔ 1.2m FLOWERING ❋ JUL-OCT
POSITION ☀ FULL SUN ☀ PARTIAL SHADE HARDINESS 3 4 5 6 **7**

Black-eyed Susan
Rudbeckia hirta

Black-eyed Susan can flower from mid-summer to the first frost, though is a short-lived perennial (2–3yrs) so will need replacing. Sits perfectly amongst grasses and really enhances a natural meadow. Prefers a heavier but well-drained soil.

HEIGHT ↕ 0.7m SPREAD ↔ 0.5m FLOWERING ❋ JUL-OCT
POSITION ☀ FULL SUN HARDINESS 3 4 5 6 **7**

Bee balm
Monarda 'Squaw'

Clump-forming deciduous perennial with mid-green lemony aromatic leaves. Prefers soils that are not too damp or too dry and that retain moisture throughout the summer. The distinctive flowerhead sits beautifully amongst grasses; even once it has dried it carries on looking great.

HEIGHT ↕ 1m SPREAD ↔ 0.6m FLOWERING ❋ JUL-SEP
POSITION ☀ FULL SUN ☀ PARTIAL SHADE HARDINESS 3 **4** 5 6 7

Sweet coneflower
Rudbeckia subtomentosa 'Henry Eilers'

Fine-quilled ray florets surround a central orangy-brown cone. The finely detailed petals create a hazy atmosphere when planted en masse, providing a pure yellow display into autumn.

HEIGHT ↕ 1.2m SPREAD ↔ 0.6m FLOWERING ❋ AUG-OCT
POSITION ☀ FULL SUN ☀ PARTIAL SHADE HARDINESS 3 4 5 6 **7**

SCHEMATIC PLANTING DESIGN

CONCEPT DESIGN

An overall colour scheme of pinks and purples

Strong direction and flow to be provided by contrasting colours

Individual plants to provide more subtle texture and detail within beds

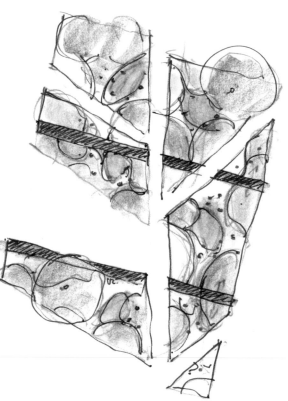

CONCEPT DEVELOPMENT

Look at proportions of plants within each planting bed

Look to run plants through the topiary hedge, unifying the beds

Orange and yellow used for the directional planting, plus contrasting yet complementary colours

FINAL PLANTING PLAN

Shows the relationships between the individual species combining to create a prairie-style planting scheme

Briza media

Sanguisorba 'Red Thunder'

Agastache foeniculum

Phlomis tuberosa 'Amazone'

Rudbeckia 'Henry Eilers'

Persicaria amplexicaulis 'Firetail'

Aster 'Monte Cassino'

Allium sphaerocephalon

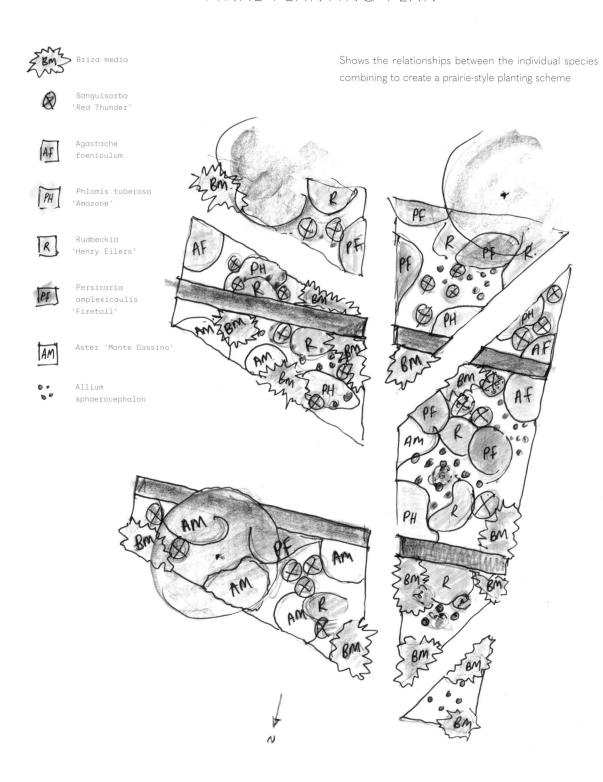

DESIGN A MEADOW

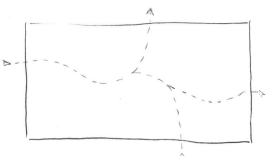

1: CHOOSE YOUR SPOT + REMOVE EXISTING VEGETATION

It's best to choose somewhere open and sunny but the ground can be flat or sloping.

For small areas you can try removing weeds by hand or else cover with black plastic for at least 3–4 months prior to sowing. For large areas non-chemical control may not be effective. In this case spray off the existing vegetation (unless it is already species-rich!) using residual systemic glyphosate-containing weedkiller.

Start to plan the paths though the meadow.

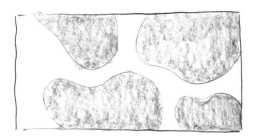

2: REMOVE SOIL FERTILITY + CREATE A SEED BED

It's best to remove the topsoil, although this does require a machine. An alternative is to put the land down to oil seed rape or mustard for a season to reduce fertility, but make sure you remove the crop at flowering time.

Remove the top 8–15cm of topsoil. Firm and rake the soil to create a fine breadcrumb-like tilth.

Retain and mow existing vegetation for the paths, though you may have to re-seed if it gets damaged.

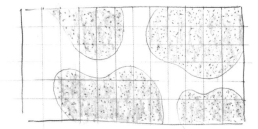

3: SOWING THE SEED

This is best done in autumn. Different seed mixes may vary but as a rule of thumb your seed mix should be sown at a mix of 5g per sq m.

Mix the seed with dry silver sand. This not only makes it easier to handle but you can easily see what ground you have covered (don't use builder's sand). The correct ratio is 3–5 parts sand to 1 of seed. Using a string grid can help even distribution of seed.

Walk gently over the ground to make sure the seeds are in contact with the soil, water thoroughly and leave them to grow naturally. Be ready to protect with a net if birds might be a problem.

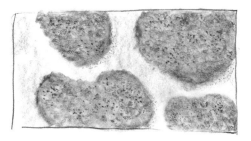

4: CUTTING THE MEADOW

In the first growing season cut the growth in midsummer and remove all dead material. In subsequent seasons, cut your meadow for hay in late June/early July. If some plants begin to dominate, vary the time of cutting each year.

Cut your hay in dry weather, using shears or a scythe. Leave it lying for up to a week, allowing seeds to drop, then clear it away for compost.

You may need to do some spot weeding to remove things like nettles, docks and thistles, but unless they are dominating there's no harm in keeping a few.

PLANTING CONTAINER-GROWN PERENNIALS

1: PREPARE

Dig over the soil and remove any weeds. When creating a new bed we recommend double digging.

2: TEASE

Remove the plant from its pot and check the roots. Sometimes these wrap around inside the pot, encircling the compost. Teasing these out with your fingers will encourage them to spread into the surrounding soil.

3: DIG

Using a spade or trowel create a hole just large enough to place the rootball in. Bury only the earth-covered roots of the plant, leaving the stems or shoots above ground.

4: REFILL

Fill the soil back in around the plant, firming it down with your hands and heels if necessary.

5: WATER

Even if the surface is already moist make sure you water in the plant as this will help settle the soil. You can also apply an organic mulch or well-rotted manure on top of the soil.

CUTTING BACK PERENNIALS

You can cut back your perennials in autumn after they have flowered to help keep the garden tidy, though we would highly recommend leaving it until March, just before the shoots begin to grow in early spring. This will preserve the seedheads and stems, providing amazing structural winter interest plus food and habitats for wildlife. It can be worth selectively cutting back in autumn, removing parts of the plants with any signs of decay or fungal growth.

Remove the stems by cutting them close to the dormant top of the plant. Avoid cutting new shoots.

DIVIDING PERENNIALS

WHY

Dividing perennials ensures a healthy plant and allows you to multiply your stock for free. Here are the general rules of dividing, though some plants do require a different method. It's best to check before you start.

WHEN

There is no specific age at which you should divide your plant, though a good rule of thumb is to do it in the autumn after the plant has looked its best. Perennials can, however, be divided at any time of the year providing they are well watered afterwards, though the process is most succesful when the plant is not actively growing.

1: LIFT

Dig up the clump of perennials by inserting the shovel deep into the soil around the perimeter to loosen roots and isolate the plant. This can be hard sometimes and may require an additional fork to help lever the plant apart.

2: REMOVE

Lever the clump out of the soil with a spade/fork. Once out of the ground shake off the excess soil around the roots, making them easier to pull apart.

3: SEPARATE

Pry or cut apart individual crowns. Make sure each clump has sets of leaves and roots.

4: REPLANT

It's best to replant the individual crowns as soon as possible so they don't dry out. Plant at the same depth as before removed and water well.

PLANTING BULBS

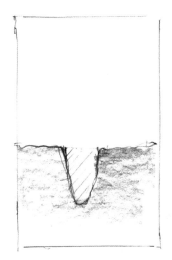 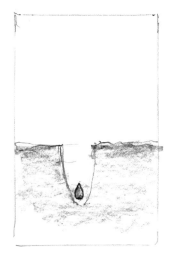 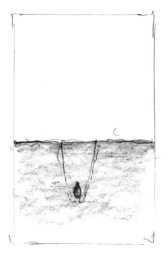

1: DIG
Dig the hole wide and deep enough for the specific bulb. A rough tip for the depth required is to measure the bulb from top to bottom and triple it.

2: NOSE UP
Place the bulb in the hole nose facing up. Space them at least two bulb widths apart.

3: REFILL
Refill the soil back into the hole and firm gently.

WHEN

AUTUMN
Plant spring-flowering bulbs by the end of September through to November (depending on climate).

SPRING
Plant tender summer bulbs at the end of March (early spring).

SUMMER
Plant autumn-flowering bulbs by August (end of summer).

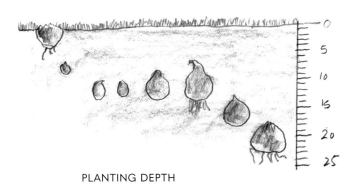

PLANTING DEPTH

IDENTIFYING YOUR SOIL TYPE

WHY

It's important to know your soil type so that you can buy the correct plants and continue to grow them in good health. Soil type means simply identifying the presence of clay, sand and silt within your soil.

HOW

The easiest way is to grab a handful, touch it and roll it around in your fingers. Sandy soil will have a gritty texture. You can feel the small grains and it won't compact into a ball. If it is a sandy loam it may stick together a little. Clay soil has a smoother, smeary quality. You can roll it into a ball much more easily and it gets slimy when wet. If rubbed with your fingers heavy clays go shiny, though lighter ones less so.

CLAY SOIL

is very fertile and can provide your plants with lots of nutrients as long as these can be broken down by adding organic matter. Clay soil warms up slowly in spring, bakes dry in summer and is wet and cold in winter.

SANDY SOIL

is free-draining and usually low in nutrients. To improve nutrient and water content add in organic matter. Sandy soil is light, dry and warms up quickly. Often acidic.

SILT SOIL

is made from fine particles that are light and free-draining but moisture-retentive and fertile. It can easily become compacted.

LOAM SOIL

is the perfect soil type comprised of the right percentages of clay, sand and silt. Loam drains well, is worked easily and is full of nutrients. As the soil has a light, open structure it heats up quickly in spring.

PEAT SOIL

is high in organic matter yet low in nutrients. Holds plenty of moisture which can cause it to become waterlogged. Peat soil is acidic.

CHALK SOIL

is stony and free-draining and can be light or heavy. Minerals such as iron and magnesium can quickly leach out so regularly adding organic fertiliser is recommended. Chalk soil is alkaline.

IMPROVING YOUR SOIL

WHY

Improving the soil really means altering its texture and structure to make it easier for roots to grow, providing the plant with all the food it needs. This is achieved by adding organic matter into the soil. Organic matter is also referred to as soil improver and soil conditioner.

WHEN

Apply organic matter in the spring, before new growth begins. Avoid using it in late summer/autumn as the nutrients may be lost over winter.

STAGE ONE

Dig well-rotted organic matter into your soil. Apply about 5–10kg per square metre. It is worth checking the weight carefully while the organic matter is dry, as wet manures and garden composts will be heavier than drier materials.

STAGE TWO

Apply about a handful of general organic fertiliser such as blood, bone and fishmeal into the soil.

TYPES OF ORGANIC MATTER

MANURE

The quality can vary according to the animals and the farming system. Don't apply when fresh; allow it to mature for a year. After a year it should have broken down so that it's black, crumbly and sweet-smelling with no visible straw.

LEAF MOULD

If the leaves are fresh and shredded just moisten, but if they are whole and dry add in some garden soil. Leave for up to two years to break down.

COMPOSTED BARK

Available in most garden centres. Holds moisture well without going boggy. Bark chippings can also be used as a mulch.

MUSHROOM COMPOST

Can be acquired in bulk from local mushroom farms, soil and manure suppliers. It is alkaline so best to alternate this with well-rotted manure/garden compost. (Not to be used on acid-loving plants.)

GARDEN COMPOST

Very cheap and convenient choice. Can make it yourself in a compost heap or bin using your kitchen and garden waste. Exclude cooked food, meat, bread, etc. from your compost, to avoid attracting rats.

"... We spent a morning trying to find a route through the pines to the coast. Some paths were more successful than others! ..."

"... Harry and Jackson enjoying the slow pace of life ...
playing pine-cone pétanque became the main
activity of the afternoon ..."

"... We love playing music. Harry has his
trumpet and Dave plays his guitar,
though rarely on such an idyllic seat ..."

COASTAL

"*Every year we embark on a road trip down to the south-west coast of France, with our surfboards, wetsuits and sleeping bags. By day we surf and at night we camp wild in the straggly pine forests or on the vast empty beaches, gazing at clear night skies and listening to waves crashing onto the constantly reforming shore.*"

Indefinably wild, an expanse of raw power that is always constant, coastlines exert relentless dominance, an authority that has shaped the land for millions of years. The harsh effects of wind, salt and sand combine to create very tough conditions; coast has the capacity to be calm and forgiving or hard and inflexible. It's this unpredictability that makes the landscape bordering the sea so fascinating.

COASTAL HABITATS IN THE UK

MARITIME CLIFFS

Maritime cliffs are the steep slopes created by erosion and slippage of land. These cliffs are defined by the geology of the surrounding area, falling broadly into two categories: hard cliffs and soft cliffs.

Hard cliffs have a more vertical slope and are formed from sandstone, limestone, granite or sometimes chalk. Due to the impenetrable nature of the rock these cliffs support fewer varieties of plants due to the shortage of areas where soil is able to collect.

Soft cliffs are composed of less resistant rock, such as shales, and unconsolidated materials like boulder clay. These cliffs are less stable and therefore form a more gentle gradient, allowing plants to colonise more easily. Many factors control the amount of vegetation on maritime cliffs: exposure to wind and salt, the composition and stability of the rock, its water content and the length of time since the last movement of the land.

COASTAL FEATURES FORMED BY EROSION

CAVES occur when waves force themselves into cracks in the cliff face. Hydraulic action gradually turns these fissures into hollow spaces.

ARCHES/SEA STACKS occur if a cave is created on a headland. Over time the waves break through to form an arch. This will gradually widen until the top collapses, leaving a stack.

WAVE-CUT PLATFORMS occur when destructive waves undercut the cliff face, creating a wave-cut notch. The cliff then collapses to create a platform.

MARITIME CLIFF VEGETATION

Ledges on hard cliffs can support
Rock samphire Crithmum maritimum
Rock sea spurrey Spergularia rupicola (in the south)
and **Scots lovage** Ligusticum scoticum (in the north).

Grasses such as
Red fescue Festuca rubra
and species such as
Thrift Armeria maritima
Sea plantain Plantago maritima
Buck's-horn plantain Plantago coronopus and
Sea carrot Daucus carota ssp. gummifer.

SALTMARSHES

SALTMARSHES are coastal wetlands situated between land and open saltwater. As they are in the upper vegetated portions of intertidal mudflats they are constantly flooded and then drained by the movement of the tide.

Saltmarshes are usually restricted to relatively sheltered areas within estuaries, beach plains, saline lagoons, behind barrier islands and at the heads of sea lochs.

Saltmarsh vegetation is restricted to salt-tolerant species adapted to regular immersion.

PIONEER SALTMARSH

Common cordgrass
Spartina anglica

Herbaceous seepweed
Suaeda maritima

Sea aster
Aster tripolium

LOW/MID SALTMARSH

Common saltmarsh-grass
Puccinellia maritima

Saltbush
Atriplex portulacoides

MID/UPPER SALTMARSH

Red fescue
Festuca rubra

Blackgrass
Juncus gerardii

Autumn hawkbit
Scorzoneroides autumnalis

Sea rush
Juncus maritimus

Chestnut sedge
Blysmus rufus

DRIFT LINE

Sea couch grass
Elytrigia atherica

Couch grass
Elytrigia repens

Alkali seepweed
Suaeda vera

COASTAL DUNES

WIND

Coastal dunes form within the intertidal zone (area above water at low tide and below water at high tide) and where onshore winds are prevalent. Some of the largest dune systems in the UK are found in the Western Isles and Inner Hebrides.

Coastal dunes are difficult places for plants to colonise due to the large expanses of bare, open, highly mobile sand. Pioneer plants such as sea holly and sea spurge are able to root on more sheltered sides of the dunes but when the dune system stabilises and decaying vegetation and manure are mixed with the sand, the variety of plant life increases.

SAND DUNE SUCCESSION

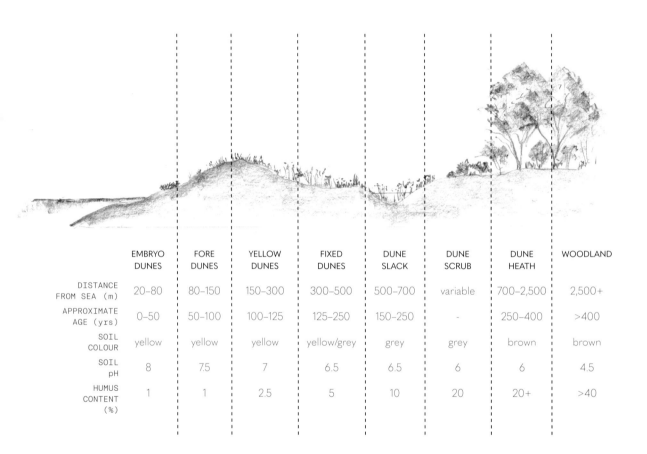

	EMBRYO DUNES	FORE DUNES	YELLOW DUNES	FIXED DUNES	DUNE SLACK	DUNE SCRUB	DUNE HEATH	WOODLAND
DISTANCE FROM SEA (m)	20–80	80–150	150–300	300–500	500–700	variable	700–2,500	2,500+
APPROXIMATE AGE (yrs)	0–50	50–100	100–125	125–250	150–250	-	250–400	>400
SOIL COLOUR	yellow	yellow	yellow	yellow/grey	grey	grey	brown	brown
SOIL pH	8	7.5	7	6.5	6.5	6	6	4.5
HUMUS CONTENT (%)	1	1	2.5	5	10	20	20+	>40

Vegetation succession is the evolution of plant communities at a site over time, from pioneer species to climax vegetation. At each stage of succession the plant communities alter the soil and microclimate enough to allow the establishing of other plants. One community of plants is replaced as the succession progresses. Eventually a climax community is reached where the plants are in a state of equilibrium with the environment.

EMBRYO DUNES/ FORE DUNES	Poor water retention	Waxy leaves to retain moisture	Sandwort *Honckenya peploides*
	Onshore winds	Low-growing to avoid wind	Saltwort *Batis maritima*
	Sand build-up	Deep tap roots to obtain moisture	Sea rocket *Cakile maritima*
	Transient dunes	High salt tolerance	Frosted orache *Atriplex laciniata*
			Sea crouch *Elytrigia atherica*
YELLOW DUNES	Reduced winds	Salt-tolerant	Marram grass *Ammophila arenaria*
	More water retention	Thrives on being buried by sand	Ragwort *Senecio jacobaea*
	Above high tide	Involuted leaves to retain moisture	Sand sedge *Carex arenaria*
	Transient dunes	Long tap roots to obtain moisture	
		Underground rhizomes stabilise sand	
FIXED DUNES	Less exposed	Lower salt tolerence	Buck's-horn plantain *Plantago coronopus*
	Stabilised sand	Higher species diversity	Viper's bugloss *Echium vulgare*
	Higher humus layer	Mainly perennials	Red fescue *Festuca rubra*
	Closed vegetation community in which marram grass can no longer compete.		Yorkshire fog *Holcus lanatus*
			Pyramidal orchid *Anacamptis pyramidalis*
DUNE SLACKS	Low-lying hollows between dunes	Moisture-loving	Flag iris *Iris pseudacorus*
	High water table	Low salt tolerence	Sea rush *Juncus maritimus*
			Bog cotton *Eriophorum angustifolium*
			Common reed *Phragmites australis*
DUNE SCRUB/ DUNE HEATH/ WOODLAND	Well sheltered	Woody perennials	Heather *Calluna vulgaris*
	Minimal salt	Understorey species	Sea buckthorn *Hippophae rhamnoides*
	Nutrient-rich	Shrubs/trees	Common gorse *Ilex europaeus*
	High organic matter		Pine *Pinus*
			Oak *Quercus robur*

ELEMENT
SIZE

Often characterised by steep cliffs and rocky outcrops the scale of the coastline can feel overwhelming. Its geological structures make magnificent natural sculptures and the adjacent sea provides a sense of unlimited space.

When recreating the character of a coastline look to add both vertical and horizontal lines. Coastlines are often enclosed to one side by high cliffs, and it's this vertical presence that can make a beach feel narrow and confined. Trees, topiary and walls can help to replicate this impression.

Softer, more reclined dunes and the wide open sea provide a feeling of calm and balance. The lack of vertical form creates a rolling space

The balance between the size of the cliffs and the size of the beach can create very different feelings, and this principle can be adopted for use in a garden design. The presence of a large, dominant object with a narrow space below it will produce an intimate and enclosed effect, whereas a larger, more open space in relation to the same object will produce a more harmonious and balanced scheme.

When you look to create a seating area within your garden think about the size of the area in relation to the surrounding objects, such as trees, architecture and boundaries.

Steep cliffs and a narrow rocky beach make this cove feel very private and enclosed

High tide gives the appearance of a larger beach. It creates a balance between the relative sizes of cliff and beach

Within this chapter we are aproaching the coast as a single habitat, combining inspiration from cliff, saltmarsh and dune habitats.

PRINCIPLE
CONTRAST

Soft carpet-like plants contrast with the harsh rocky tracks, highlighting a route down to the sea

Coastline is an amalgamation of different materials and textures, often with two contrasting materials meeting in an unsympathetic way. The fine texture of sand forms a muted surface that contrasts with the rocky outcrops and vegetation. It allows your eye to be drawn to the more obvious forms and textures in the surrounding landscape.

Within a garden, look to use a muted material on the ground. Surfaces such as gravel and concrete can be quite subtle, contrasting with the busier planting and other more textured materials.

Rippled sand leads the eye on to the contrasting forms of the boulders and towards the treeline

This coastline displays three contrasting textures: the minimal, light, coloured sea; the more complex, craggy rock, and the soft, feathery planting

SINGLE-STEMMED PINE PROVIDES
A DAPPLED CANOPY WITHOUT
BLOCKING OUT THE SPACE

BOULDERS CREATE
A NATURAL FEATURE
WITHIN THE SPACE

SHALLOW-WATER POOL

L-SHAPED BENCH CREATES A MORE
INTIMATE SEATING ARRANGEMENT

INSPIRATION

In the design individual concrete pads keep the same minimal texture as the sand whilst allowing planting between them, echoing the low grass on the dunes.

Natural boulders sit within the pool below the wall, shaded by a single-stemmed pine. This area creates a tranquil and relaxing point of interest to look at from the designed bench. A low rendered wall frames the bench, creating an intimate area from which to look back over the garden, also reducing the impact of the wind.

Isolating individual colours from a coastal habitat will help to inspire a colour scheme within your garden. This aerial photograph provides a wide range of coastal colours that could be used to decide a wall colour, the type of wood for decking, what gravel to use on a path and the tones of your planting scheme.

DESIGN CONCEPTS

CONTRAST OF SPACE

Topiary 'sea stacks' subtly define individual spaces within the garden. Their shadows provide ever-changing detail throughout the day.

A curved lawn represents the shoreline.

Taller trees on the left-hand boundary give the illusion of cliffs, providing intimacy and scale within the garden.

Sawn paving creates the walkway and represents the beach within the design. A sawn sandstone or limestone would create a modern, clean finish in the garden.

Large irregular topiary domes have been positioned throughout the space, representing sea stacks. We have used them to create a physical connection between the individual spaces by breaking the lines between planting and slabbing, and paving and lawn.

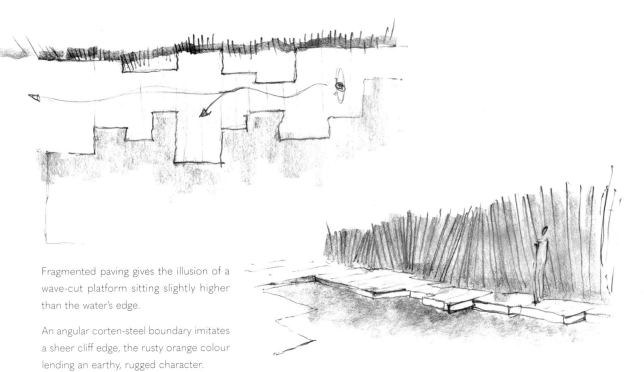

Fragmented paving gives the illusion of a wave-cut platform sitting slightly higher than the water's edge.

An angular corten-steel boundary imitates a sheer cliff edge, the rusty orange colour lending an earthy, rugged character.

Designed to capture the feeling of a walk through the pines to the beach, a wooden boardwalk leads through a concentration of pine and oak to a more open space with a focal water feature.

The planting amongst the trees is soft and fluid, made up predominantly of grasses.

A topiary wall on the back boundary has been shaped to give the appearance of waves.

FLUID MOVEMENT

Inspired by waves. Their strong horizontal forms can be transcribed into walls.

This splits the garden into individual rooms whilst breaking the eyeline, giving the illusion that the garden is larger than it is.

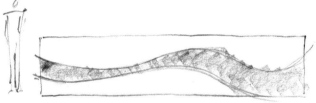

Inspired by rock strata revealed on eroded coastlines, concrete can be poured in different ways to create contrasting textures and shapes within a wall.

The lower and upper layers are a wetter mix, forming a tighter, smoother finish, whereas the centre layer is a much drier consistency. This allows air pockets to form, giving a rougher, more rustic finish.

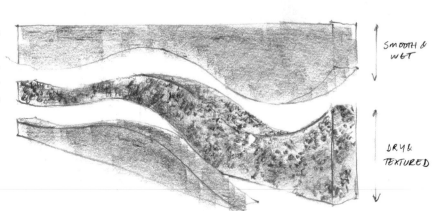

SMOOTH & WET

DRY & TEXTURED

FLUID MOVEMENT

Large drifts of grasses either side of a dune-shaped landform provide a sense of movement.

WAVE MOVEMENT

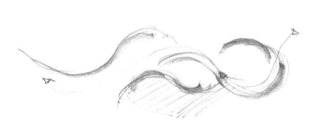

This design concept has been inspired by the movement and shape of waves. We have used low hedging to elevate the wave pattern, defining a route through the garden.

The main body of the garden is made up of planting. This will emulate the movement of the sea and provide changes of interest throughout the seasons.

Multi-stemmed trees provide vertical interest, obscuring views and enclosing the space within a dappled canopy.

ROCKS + ROCK POOLS

A design inspired by the route water takes when running into rock pools at high tide. In the garden, 'rock pools' create pockets of interest along a meandering path.

A gravel path planted with lines of low-lying planting simulates the meandering character of water on a beach.

The same concept as above but with lines of low planting leading from a land mound and cutting across the direction of the path.

You could use poured concrete to create a cleaner, more modern-looking slab.

Imitating the layout of coastal rock pools can provide
design inspiration. Shading in individual spaces creates
islands and potential seating areas.

The developed scheme begins to form individual planting
beds, leaving a central open space for seating.

The repeated forms of the beds create tracks through the
garden. Walls add further definition and lead towards the
more usable space in the centre.

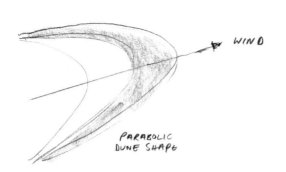

PARABOLIC
DUNE SHAPE

WIND

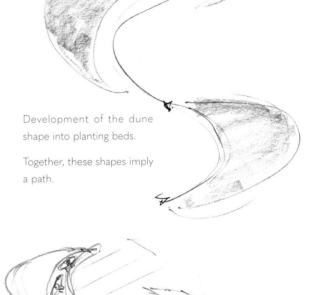

Development of the dune shape into planting beds.

Together, these shapes imply a path.

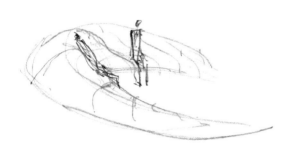

The same dune shape could be used as landform. This could be further developed into seating.

An amphitheatre arrangement creates an enclosed space protected from the elements. A social shape, encouraging interaction.

Using two landforms positioned opposite each other forms a connection that also encourages interaction.

Dune shape could outline a path. The undulating land prompts an interesting journey through the garden.

Planting can give the same illusion of height that a landform provides, but is less interactive and creates a more defined boundary.

A COASTAL GARDEN

INITIAL CONCEPT

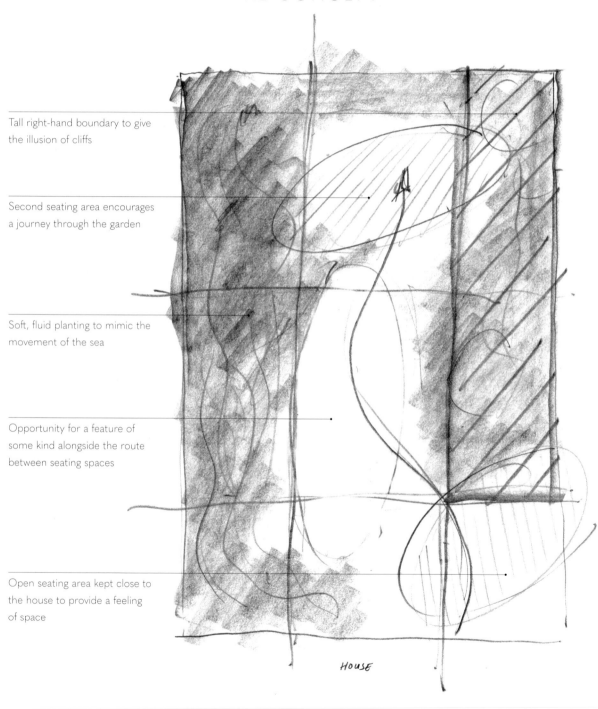

Tall right-hand boundary to give
the illusion of cliffs

Second seating area encourages
a journey through the garden

Soft, fluid planting to mimic the
movement of the sea

Opportunity for a feature of
some kind alongside the route
between seating spaces

Open seating area kept close to
the house to provide a feeling
of space

HOUSE

CONCEPT DEVELOPMENT

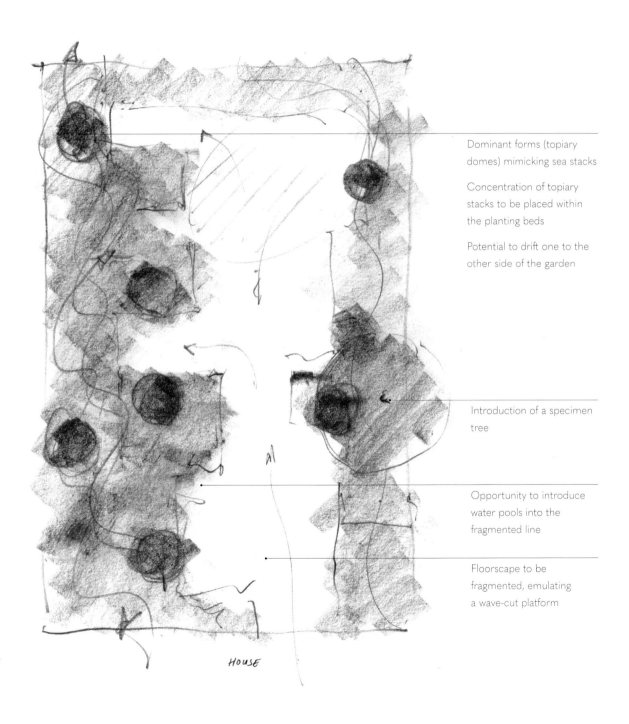

Dominant forms (topiary domes) mimicking sea stacks

Concentration of topiary stacks to be placed within the planting beds

Potential to drift one to the other side of the garden

Introduction of a specimen tree

Opportunity to introduce water pools into the fragmented line

Floorscape to be fragmented, emulating a wave-cut platform

HOUSE

CONCEPT DEVELOPMENT

Collection of trees and shrubs on the right-hand boundary providing height within the garden

Specimen tree positioned top left to create a balance with the trees opposite

The garden has been divided into three distinct spaces. Rougher stone runs from the pools, providing a varied experience when walking across

Pools' area determined by the fragmented shape of the floor

Linear stones sit within the water features, creating a natural detail inspired by rock pools

Decking has been used to give a more coastal character

The decking will create warmer, more comfortable areas in the site while the direction of the decking boards will help draw the eye to the end of the garden, giving an impression of length

HOUSE

FINAL DESIGN

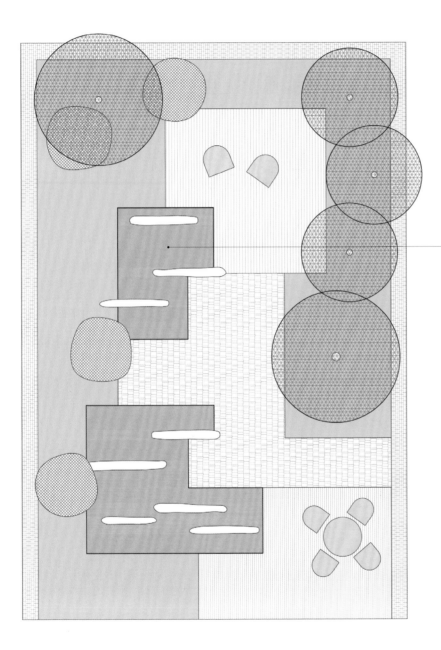

Only minor alterations were
found to be necessary when
finalising the design

Slightly adapted positions
of stones to create a more
balanced feature within the
water

FINAL DESIGN VISUALS

Due to the shape of the stone features within the pools, two different visual effects are created. From both seating areas they appear a more dominant form, though when walking beside them they appear less dominant, drawing the focus over the water and towards the planting behind.

The textured stone on the ground splits the garden into two. We wanted to set the direction of the stone against that of the decking to create a stronger connection with the stone in the pools.

From this aspect the topiary stacks appear to be the dominant forms within the garden.

TEXTURED STONE ON THE GROUND

The topiary stacks appear less dominant from this aspect. The layering of stone within the pools and tall naturalistic planting softens the overall effect.

A dining space is positioned nearer the house, making it accessible and practical.

The more informal seating is positioned at the far end of the garden, encouraging you to travel through the space. Positioning it here helps to detach it from the house, making it a quiet spot to relax in.

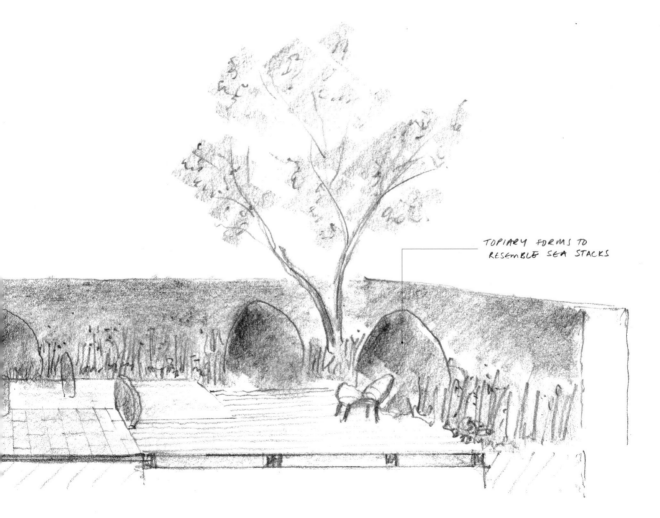

TOPIARY FORMS TO RESEMBLE SEA STACKS

COASTAL PLANTING

Coastal conditions are very challenging, so when a plant is able to survive in a certain area it's likely that it will multiply. Low-lying robust plants cling to the sand whilst grasses emerge from the dunes *en masse*, moving in the wind and accentuating the mounded landform.

Within your garden large drifts of grasses provide a natural dune-like character. Their light feathery heads sway in the wind and their late summer oaty colour picks up the tones of the sand.

Coastal trees and shrubs appear more rugged and isolated. The constant beating they endure from the elements can provide them with a gnarled and characterful appearance. Choosing the correct species such as hawthorn, tamarisk and pine will dramatically alter the atmosphere of your garden.

IMITATING A NATIVE COASTAL SCHEME

SALT-TOLERANT PLANTS

EMBRYO/ FORE DUNES

Low-lying, waxy,

creeping plants:

Sea lavender
Limonium latifolium

Lambs' ears
Stachys byzantina
'Silver Carpet'

Ice plant
Sedum spectabile
'Stardust'

Sea thistle
Eryngium maritimum

Broad-leaved statice
Limonium platyphyllum

YELLOW DUNES

Tall grasses:

Feather-reed grass
Calamagrostis x acutiflora
'Karl Foerster'

GREY DUNES

Low grasses,

perennial varieties:

Red fescue
Festuca rubra

Yarrow
Achillea millefolium

Horned poppy
Glaucium flavum

DUNE HEATH/ WOODLAND

Shrubs, trees:

Black pine
Pinus nigra

Sea buckthorn
Hippophae rhamnoides

SALT-TOLERANT PLANTING SCHEME

PLANTING DESIGN CONCEPT

Trees and shrubs on the perimeter of the design, enclosing the space

Landform provides the appearance of sand dunes

The journey is kept undefined, imitating a sandy track

Low-lying textured planting evokes a coastal character

Large drifts of grasses

DEVELOPED PLANTING DESIGN

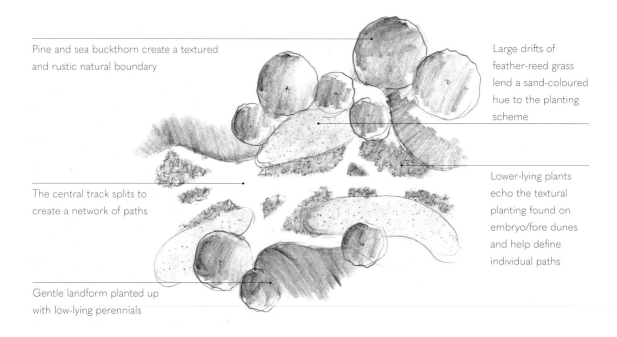

Pine and sea buckthorn create a textured and rustic natural boundary

Large drifts of feather-reed grass lend a sand-coloured hue to the planting scheme

The central track splits to create a network of paths

Lower-lying plants echo the textural planting found on embryo/fore dunes and help define individual paths

Gentle landform planted up with low-lying perennials

SALT-TOLERANT

PERENNIALS

Rosemary
Rosmarinus officinalis

A woody perennial herb, evergreen with narrow aromatic leaves. Flowers in spring and again at varying times throughout the summer. Its scent and robust character provoke a strong Mediterranean feeling.

HEIGHT ↕ 1.5m SPREAD ↔ 1.5m FLOWERING ✻ MAY-JUL
POSITION ☀ FULL SUN HARDINESS 3 **4** 5 6 7

Yarrow
Achillea millefolium

Found growing wild in grasslands, this hardy perennial has a high salt tolerance. Its soft fern-like leaves provide a mat-forming ground cover and small white flowers attract insects. A great plant to dot amongst grasses for a naturalistic feeling.

HEIGHT ↕ 0.9m SPREAD ↔ 0.3m FLOWERING ✻ MAY-AUG
POSITION ☀ FULL SUN HARDINESS 3 4 5 6 **7**

Lady's mantle
Alchemilla mollis

Looks good en masse when its leaves froth and merge together. It's perfect for softening a path or front of border and produces tiny clusters of yellow flowers which seed freely. Can tolerate most soil conditions and light shade.

HEIGHT ↕ 0.6m SPREAD ↔ 0.75m FLOWERING ✻ JUN-SEP
POSITION ☀ FULL SUN ⛅ PARTIAL SHADE HARDINESS 3 4 5 6 **7**

Flowering sea kale
Crambe cordifolia

Produces large dark green leaves and a cloud of airy white flowers. This perennial looks great at the back of a sunny border. A statement plant providing long spells of interest. Requires free-draining soil and a more sheltered spot.

HEIGHT ↕ 1.5m SPREAD ↔ 1.5m FLOWERING ✻ JUN-JUL
POSITION ☀ FULL SUN ⛅ PARTIAL SHADE HARDINESS 3 4 **5** 6 7

SALT-TOLERANT

PERENNIALS

Miss Willmott's ghost

Eryngium giganteum

An attractive architectural plant. Its spiny leaves and blue flowerheads make this a real statement in your scheme. Tough and robust so can handle exposed sites. Prefers a sandy or loam soil that is well drained.

HEIGHT ↕ 0.5m SPREAD ↔ 0.45m FLOWERING ❋ JUL-SEP
POSITION ☼ FULL SUN HARDINESS 3 4 5 6 7

Red valerian

Centranthus ruber

Dense pink/red clusters of fragrant star-shaped florets. This semi-evergreen woody-based perennial sits well in a wild planting scheme, self-seeds freely and is useful to wildlife. Prefers a well-drained sand, loam or chalk soil. Perfect for an exposed site.

HEIGHT ↕ 0.8m SPREAD ↔ 0.45m FLOWERING ❋ JUL-OCT
POSITION ☼ FULL SUN HARDINESS 3 4 5 6 7

Blue globe thistle

Echinops bannaticus

Large blue globe-shaped flowerheads with pinnate lobed leaves. It provides a naturalistic look and is best planted in drifts to provide a vivid display. Seedheads look good in winter as they provide texture and structure. Prefers a poorer soil that is well drained.

HEIGHT ↕ 1.5m SPREAD ↔ 0.6m FLOWERING ❋ JUL-AUG
POSITION ☼ FULL SUN HARDINESS 3 4 5 6 7

Lambs' ears

Stachys byzantina 'Big Ears'

Large evergreen felted leaves create the perfect ground cover to suppress weeds. Tolerates drought and thrives in sand, loam and chalk soils as long as they are free-draining.

HEIGHT ↕ 0.45m SPREAD ↔ 0.6m FLOWERING ❋ JUN-SEP
POSITION ☼ FULL SUN HARDINESS 3 4 5 6 7

3 hardy in coastal and relatively mild parts of the UK [-5 to 1°C]
4 hardy through most of the UK [-10 to -5°C]
5 hardy in most places throughout the UK, even in severe winters [-15 to -10°C]
6 hardy in all of UK and northern Europe [-20 to -15°C]
7 hardy in the severest European continental climates [-20°C and lower]

SALT-TOLERANT

PERENNIALS

Turkish sage

Phlomis russeliana

Large ovate textured leaves create a strong clump below stems of hooded yellow flowers. After flowering it reveals a distinctive silhouette that looks dramatic amongst grasses. Prefers a lighter, well-drained soil and can tolerate drought. Vigorous spreading perennial.

HEIGHT ↕ 0.9m SPREAD ↔ 0.75m FLOWERING ✻ MAY-SEP
POSITION ☼ FULL SUN HARDINESS 3 4 5 6 7

Stonecrop

Sedum 'Autumn Joy'

Clump-forming perennial revealing pink clusters of star-shaped flowers on sturdy stems. Succulent, evergreen foliage provides good structure within your scheme and a winter silhouette. The perfect filler plant for a sunny border. Pollinators love it.

HEIGHT ↕ 0.6m SPREAD ↔ 0.6m FLOWERING ✻ AUG-SEP
POSITION ☼ FULL SUN ◐ PARTIAL SHADE HARDINESS 3 4 5 6 7

Field scabious

Scabiosa columbaria

Beautifully delicate perennial with light blue/purple flowerheads, narrow stems and simple lobed leaves. Tolerates most soil conditions and exposed sites.

HEIGHT ↕ 1.5m SPREAD ↔ 0.3m FLOWERING ✻ JUL-SEP
POSITION ☼ FULL SUN HARDINESS 3 4 5 6 7

Giant silver mullein

Verbascum bombyciferum

A strong architectural plant with semi-evergreen leaves and tall flower stalks. A biennial that is great for drought conditions, it will self-seed but not uncontrollably. Prefers poorer, well-drained soil.

HEIGHT ↕ 1.8m SPREAD ↔ 0.6m FLOWERING ✻ JUL-AUG
POSITION ☼ FULL SUN HARDINESS 3 4 5 6 7

SALT-TOLERANT

GRASSES

Red fescue

Festuca rubra

A fine-leaved perennial grass that can grow in dense tufts or spread to form patches. Requires very little maintenance, tolerates dry shade and will stay almost evergreen if not cut down.

HEIGHT ↕ 0.3m SPREAD ↔ 0.25m FLOWERING ✻ JUN-JUL
POSITION ☼ FULL SUN HARDINESS ③ ④ ❺ ⑥ ⑦

Feather-reed grass

Calamagrostis × acutiflora 'Karl Foerster'

A clump-forming, upright grass bearing bronze flower panicles. Perfect for creating vertical structure within your scheme, whether in small groups or en masse it will add a great architectural yet natural character to your garden. Tolerates all soil types but prefers it moist but well drained.

HEIGHT ↕ 1.8m SPREAD ↔ 0.6m FLOWERING ✻ FEB/MAY
POSITION ☼ FULL SUN ◐ PARTIAL SHADE HARDINESS ③ ④ ⑤ ⑥ ❼

Fountain grass

Pennisetum alopecuroides 'Hameln'

Soft cylindrical flowerheads sit above a clump of blade-like foliage. Planted en masse these fluffy brushstroke flowers look incredible. Prefers a well-drained soil in a sheltered spot.

HEIGHT ↕ 1.2m SPREAD ↔ 1m FLOWERING ✻ JUL-SEP
POSITION ☼ FULL SUN ◐ PARTIAL SHADE HARDINESS ③ ❹ ⑤ ⑥ ⑦

Blue oat grass

Helictotrichon sempervirens

Natural and understated, this evergreen grass creates a dense silvery-blue clump of rigid leaves and produces erect arching stems revealing silver-gold spikelets. Tolerates all soil types but prefers it well drained. A tough plant, it tolerates an exposed site.

HEIGHT ↕ 1.4m SPREAD ↔ 0.6m FLOWERING ✻ JUN-JUL
POSITION ☼ FULL SUN HARDINESS ③ ④ ⑤ ⑥ ❼

SALT-TOLERANT

GRASSES

Little bluestem

Schizachyrium scoparium

A great prairie-style grass displaying blue-green foliage and vertical flowerheads, turning coppery in autumn. A deciduous grass that requires a well-drained, poor soil for best growth in the UK.

HEIGHT ↕ 1.2m SPREAD ↔ 0.6m FLOWERING ✻ FEB/AUG
POSITION ☼ FULL SUN HARDINESS 3 4 5 **6** 7

Blue fescue

Festuca glauca 'Elijah Blue'

Compact ornamental grass with blue-green flowers. A vertical structure that looks great accentuated by other blue flowers. The flowers turn a beautiful light brown in autumn, providing great seasonal interest. It has a strong Mediterranean character, especially surrounded with gravel. Great in a dry sunny spot.

HEIGHT ↕ 0.3m SPREAD ↔ 0.25m FLOWERING ✻ JUN-JUL
POSITION ☼ FULL SUN HARDINESS 3 4 **5** 6 7

Himalayan fairy grass

Miscanthus nepalensis

Arching linear green leaves are topped with soft golden spikelets. These silky, feathery flowers provide a natural detail that persists into autumn and remain architectural throughout winter. A great feature plant. Tolerates all soil types and exposed sites.

HEIGHT ↕ 1.5m SPREAD ↔ 0.8m FLOWERING ✻ MAY-JUN
POSITION ☼ FULL SUN HARDINESS 3 4 5 **6** 7

North American wild oats

Chasmanthium latifolium

A decidous spreading grass with narrow leaves and arching stems. Bears a flattened diamond-shaped flower in late summer. Tolerates all soil types as long as they are well drained.

HEIGHT ↕ 1m SPREAD ↔ 0.8m FLOWERING ✻ AUG-SEP
POSITION ☼ FULL SUN ◐ PARTIAL SHADE HARDINESS 3 4 5 6 **7**

COASTAL MEADOW
PLANTING MIX

Exposed areas of ground close to the sea can provide challanging conditions. This meadow mix includes species that will thrive in them. They are also suited to tidal and saltmarsh areas.

PRIMARY SPECIES   <70%

↑ Yorkshire fog
Holcus lanatus

Slender creeping red fescue
Festuca rubra
litoralis

Tall fescue
Festuca arundinacea

Meadow fescue
Festuca pratensis

Crested dog's tail
Cynosurus cristatus

SECONDARY SPECIES   <20%

↑ Red campion
Silene dioicia

Meadow buttercup
Ranunculus acris

Creeping bent
Agrostis stolonifera

Ribwort plantain
Plantago lanceolata

Tall oat grass
Arrhenatherum elatius

Yellow flag
Iris pseudacorus

Perennial rye grass
Lolium perenne

Wild carrot
Daucus carota
ssp. gummifer

Thrift
Armeria maritima

TERTIARY SPECIES   <10%

↑ Bird's foot trefoil
Lotus corniculatus

Dandelion
Taraxacum officinale

Red clover
Trifolium pratense

White clover
Trifolium repens

Sweet vernal grass
Anthoxanthum odoratum

Broadleaf plantain
Plantago major

Autumn hawkbit
Scorzoneroides
autumnalis

Cat's ear
Hypchaeris radicata

Tufted vetch
Vicia cracca

SALT-TOLERANT

TREES

Black pine

Pinus nigra

One of the most robust of the pines, adopting an irregular shape with age. Long dark green needles and textured bark provide a very natural character. An evergreen tree that can tolerate exposed sites and all soil types provided they are well drained.

HEIGHT ↕ up to 30m SPREAD ↔ 8m+
POSITION ☀ FULL SUN HARDINESS 3 4 5 6 **7**

Holm oak

Quercus ilex

An evergreen oak with glossy dark green leaves. Beautiful dark trunks with finely cracked bark. Great in most soils as long as they are well drained and can tolerate part shade throughout the day.

HEIGHT ↕ up to 20m SPREAD ↔ 8m+ FLOWERING ✻ JUN
POSITION ☀ FULL SUN ⛅ PARTIAL SHADE HARDINESS 3 4 **5** 6 7

Monterey cypress

Cupressus macrocarpa

Large evergreen tree becoming wider and more irregular with age. Displays erect sprays of green foliage and produces globose cones 2–3cm across.

HEIGHT ↕ up to 30m SPREAD ↔ 4m
POSITION ☀ FULL SUN HARDINESS 3 **4** 5 6 7

Common alder

Alnus glutinosa

Deciduous columnular/upright tree. Simple rounded leaves, grey-purple buds and young catkins clearly visible in winter. Can tolerate poorly drained soils and exposed sites.

HEIGHT ↕ up to 25m SPREAD ↔ 8m+
POSITION ☀ FULL SUN ⛅ PARTIAL SHADE HARDINESS 3 4 5 6 **7**

SALT-TOLERANT

SHRUBS

Hawthorn

Crataegus monogyna

A good deciduous tree for the coast as it displays the natural characteristics of an inland tree but tolerates the tough conditions. Rugged thorny stems with clusters of creamy-white flowers followed by red fruits in autumn. Tolerates most soil conditions.

HEIGHT ↕ 6m+ SPREAD ↔ 6m+ FLOWERING ❀ MAY
POSITION ☼ FULL SUN ◐ PARTIAL SHADE HARDINESS 3 4 5 6 **7**

Bay laurel

Laurus nobilis

The bay laurel is a large, aromatic evergreen shrub native to the Mediterranean. It's very happy in the ground or in a pot and can be clipped to create formal shapes. Grows in most soil conditions as long as it is free-draining. As a multi-stemmed shrub it forms a dense barrier against the prevailing wind.

HEIGHT ↕ 7m+ SPREAD ↔ 6m+ FLOWERING ❀ MAR-MAY
POSITION ☼ FULL SUN ◐ PARTIAL SHADE HARDINESS 3 **4** 5 6 7

Japanese pittosporum

Pittosporum tobira

The perfect shrub for a tricky spot. Tolerates salt, shade and drought. It can be pruned into shapes, though we prefer to let it grow naturally. Great around a seating area as it produces delicate white flowers in summer that give off a beautiful scent. This bushy evergreen shrub requires a well-drained soil.

HEIGHT ↕ 3m+ SPREAD ↔ 2m+ FLOWERING ❀ JUN-JUL
POSITION ☼ FULL SUN ◐ PARTIAL SHADE HARDINESS 3 **4** 5 6 7

Tamarisk

Tamarix ramosissima

This medium-sized deciduous arching shrub displays feathery soft pale-green foliage and small pink flowers that cover the shrub in late summer. It has a wild appearance, making it perfect for a natural coastal garden. Prefers a lighter, well-drained soil.

HEIGHT ↕ 8m+ SPREAD ↔ 8m+ FLOWERING ❀ AUG-SEP
POSITION ☼ FULL SUN HARDINESS 3 4 5 6 **7**

Concretes are self-hardening mixtures based on the use of cement as a bonding agent. Cement consists of one-third lime and one-third clay, fired to the sinter limit: at a temperature of approximately 1,400°C, what is known as Portland cement clinker is created. This is ground down to a fine dust to create Portland cement.

TYPES OF CONCRETE

REINFORCED: To increase the strength of concrete elements steel rods and/or mats are placed throughout the cross-section. This is used in structural elements such as walls and floors.

WATERTIGHT: A concrete with a high resistance to permeation, due to its granular mixture low in cavities.

SELF-COMPACTING: With a consistency similar to honey this concrete flows around obstacles and into cavities, needing no further compaction. This is ideal for casting steps, blocks or large platforms within a garden.

VACUUM CONCRETE: A process mainly used for paving slabs. Concrete is installed with a high water content, making it easier to compact, then the water is sucked out using vacuum mats and pumps. This cuts the risk of shinkage cracks and frost damage.

FIBRE: Added steel fibres are evenly distributed within the concrete, adding strength and helping to prevent cracked or broken edges. This is used a lot in the manufacturing of large cast *in situ* concrete paving slabs.

PRECAST: These are industrially produced concrete elements such as steps, coping slabs and benches.

EXPOSED: This has become very popular in garden designs. It is the process of creating a framework of coated wood or artificial panels into which you pour the concrete. Once set you remove the framework to reveal the cement structure.

SURFACE TEXTURES

Concrete is an extremely versatile material. When using it as a floorscape there are many different styles and textures you can employ, such as **coarse brushstokes**, **fine brushstrokes**, **charring**, **smoothing**, **washing**, **blasting** and **grinding**.

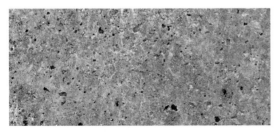

Aggregate can be mixed into the concrete to achieve this look. The concrete can be washed off to increase exposure of the aggregate.

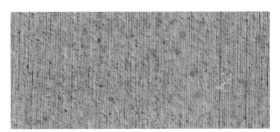

A uniform texture is achieved by strokes with a fine broom.

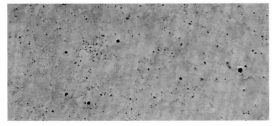

Using a concrete float produces a smooth surface texture.

Pouring concrete between a wooden framework produces an honest grained texture.

CONSTUCTING LIVING WINDBREAKS

PROBLEM

Wind can be very destructive in a coastal landscape. It breaks branches and stems, soaks up moisture causing drought stress, uproots plants and trees and strips soil from planting beds.

SOLUTION

A natural, semi-permeable windbreak on the perimeter of the garden will provide a more sheltered, calm environment within it. If you have the room then a larger, more substantial planting layer is the best option.

HOW

To create the most effective windbreak start by using the lowest of your chosen shrubs, proceeding next to the larger shubs and trees and then back down again to larger shrubs. This gives the wind a gentle gradient to pass over. It's important not to plant up this layer too densely, allowing up to 40% of the wind to filter through.

POSITIONING

Your windbreak should face the prevailing wind. It will reduce the wind on its leeward side to a distance of ten times its height, and, if possible, it's always worth making it wider than the area you are protecting as wind can get around the sides.

Take note of the topography of the land as this can affect the wind's direction. It can be funnelled between trees and through valleys, resulting in a wind tunnel, and if the ground is hilly, can be forced in a number of directions, meaning you will have to shelter the area from more than one side.

TYPICAL WINDBREAK PROFILE

WIND

MEDIUM	HIGH	MEDIUM	LOW
Dense shrubs	Tall trees	Dense shrubs	Dense shrubs

SPACING

An integral part of a windbreak is that the trees and shrubs act together as a unit. Planting the trees and shrubs too closely together can cause their effectivness to decline due to competition for light and moisture. A common issue with overly close spacing is the loss of foliage due to shading. Without all their leaves the trees' effectiveness as a windbreak declines.

	Space between trees in rows (m)	Space between rows (m)
Dense shrubs	1–2	8–10
Medium trees	3–6	4–7
Tall trees	4–7	7–9

PLANT SELECTION

An important consideration when designing your windbreak is to maximise the diversity of species. This not only provides great habitats for wildlife but reduces the risk of insect, disease or environmental problems.

SALT-TOLERANT TREES + SHRUBS FOR WINDBREAKS

HIGH

Austrian pine
Pinus nigra

Holm oak
Quercus ilex

Norway maple
Acer platanoides

Turkey oak
Quercus cerris

Monterey pine
Pinus radiata

Maritime pine
Pinus pinaster

Common alder
Alnus glutinosa

MEDIUM

Red tamarisk
Tamarix ramosissima

Blackthorn
Prunus spinosa

Sea buckthorn
Hippophae rhamnoides

Bay tree
Laurus nobilis

Ebbinge's silverberry
Elaeagnus × ebbingei

Daisy bush
Olearia × haastii

Golden elder
Sambucus nigra

Common hawthorn
Crataegus monogyna

LOW

Firethorn
Pyracantha

Shrubby hare's ear
Bupleurum fruticosum

Wilson's honeysuckle
Lonicera nitida

Eglantine
Rosa rubiginosa

Mugo pine
Pinus mugo escallonia

LESS TOLERANT + SALT-INTOLERANT TREES + SHRUBS FOR WINDBREAKS

DECIDUOUS TREES

Field maple
Acer campestre

Norway maple
Acer platanoides

Sycamore
Acer pseudoplatanus

Italian alder
Alnus cordata

Hornbeam
Carpinus betulus

Ash
Fraxinus excelsior

White poplar
Populus alba 'Pyramidalis'

Balsam poplar
Populus balsamifera

White willow
Salix alba

Whitebeam
Sorbus aria

Mountain ash
Sorbus aucuparia

Small-leaved lime
Tilia cordata

EVERGREEN TREES

Incense cedar
Calocedrus decurrens

Rocky mountain juniper
Juniperus scopulorum

Norway spruce
Picea abies

Western red cedar
Thuja plicata

LARGE/MEDIUM DECIDUOUS SHRUBS

Serviceberry
Amelanchier canadensis

Hazel
Corylus avellana

Lilac
Syringa vulgaris

Common dogwood
Cornus sanguinea

LARGE/MEDIUM EVERGREEN SHRUBS

Ebbinges silverberry
Elaeagnus × ebbingei

Juniper
Juniperus communis

Firethorn
Pyracantha

Yew
Taxus baccata

CONSTRUCTING WINDBREAKS

HAZEL HURDLES

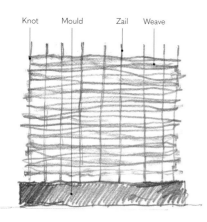

Knot   Mould   Zail   Weave

WHY

Hurdles have had many uses in the past, though by far the most popular was containing sheep within a fold. Nowadays they are used predominantly as sustainable garden screens, fencing and windbreaks.

1: MOULD

This is to stand the hurdle in whilst you are making it. You'll need a heavy piece of timber approx. 2m long (railway sleepers work perfectly).

Create 9 pairs of holes all the way through the timber approx 20cm apart. These are for the vertical rods (zails) to stand in.

Note the curved line of the holes and double series of holes to allow for variation in spacing.

2: ZAILS

Place in the zails, pushing them down into the ground so that they will stand firm when weaving around them.

3: WEAVE

Weave the horizontal rods around the nine zails. Alternate the weave each time. These can be whole rods or split in half (cleft).

Every 8–10cm higher in the hurdle the cleft rods are bent around and woven back in. This is what holds the whole construction together.

Bang down the horizontal rods as you work, keeping them tight and level.

4: KNOT

On the final top layer, commonly using a whole rod, twist this twice around the end zail then feed it back into the hurdle. This is done on both sides.

You may need to prise the horizontal rods apart to feed in the rod, then release to create a pinch, holding it in place.

5: TRIM

Cut off the tops of the zails a couple of inches above the top horizontal rod.

LIVING WILLOW SCREEN

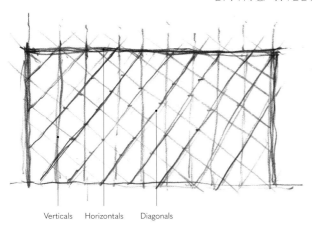

Verticals   Horizontals   Diagonals

WHY

Living willow screens work best in naturally moist and sunny spots. Willow will grow in most soils, though one that retains moisture will encourage more vigorous growth.

Willow can grow up to 2 metres a year so it may be necessary to trim it several times annually if you want to retain the original dimensions. You can trim it in winter.

1: HOLES

String out a line where you would like your willow screen.

Make holes in the ground along this line. Distance apart can vary but approx. 20cm.

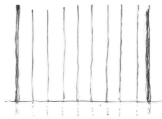

2: VERTICALS

Choose thicker, stronger rods of willow and push them into the ground, to a depth of at least 30cm.

Place 3–4 separate rods at each end for strength.

3: HORIZONTALS

Start to weave in more flexible rods at what will be the top of your screen. Form a line of between 5–10 rods, varying the weave for strength.

These will help keep the screen firm and upright. Tie in with thin strips of willow to keep them in place.

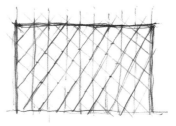

4: DIAGONALS

Start to fill in between the uprights with diagonal rods. Choose one direction first (right), then once finished complete the other direction (left). Place the diagonal rods into the soil between the uprights.

The stems may naturally graft onto each other but it's best to tie these in with thin willow as well.

Cut away the uprights above the top of the woven section.

BUILDING A WATER FEATURE

RILLS

WHY

Inspired by long channels of water left on the beach, a garden rill echoes this steady, tranquil body of water. We love the way that your eye is led down to the horizon, providing a subtle and instinctive route to follow.

Rills take up very little space; they can be used as a design feature to lead your eye down the garden or as a functional feature to move water through the garden.

They can be made with a weathered, aged look from reclaimed York stone, or given a more modern crisp character by using a sawn slab.

HOW

1: Excavate a channel from the ground. Make sure it's wide enough as you can easily backfill with the soil you removed.

2: Pour a concrete foundation at a depth of approximately 150mm. Depth is dependent on soil stability and size of rill. Leave to set.

3: Build up the concrete blocks from the foundation to the desired height of the rill. Make sure the tops of the blocks are level. When working out the final height take into account the thickness of the coping slab and the mortar course. Leave to set.

4: Lay a protective underlay within the channel and up over the blocks. Then lay your liner on top and smooth out the creases. Make sure you have excess as the weight of the water can pull the liner down very slightly. Tuck the liner behind the concrete blocks. (Using box-welded liners that come pre-made to the dimensions of your rill is a great alternative.)

5: Lay in the cable for the pump. It will sit beneath the coping slab and feed out through the stone facing. A submersible pump with a maximum flow of 4,000 litres per hour will create an appropriately gentle flow of water.

6: Build up the stone faces on top of the liner. Use little mortar between courses to achieve a dry-stone effect. Be careful not to damage the liner.

7: Measure and cut the stone slabs. Lay them within the bottom of the rill upon a shallow mortar course. Leave to set.

8: Lay your coping stone on top of a mortar course with an overhang of between 2.5–5cm. This will cast a crisp shadow onto the water.

9: Fill the rill with water. The final level should be just below that of the liner.

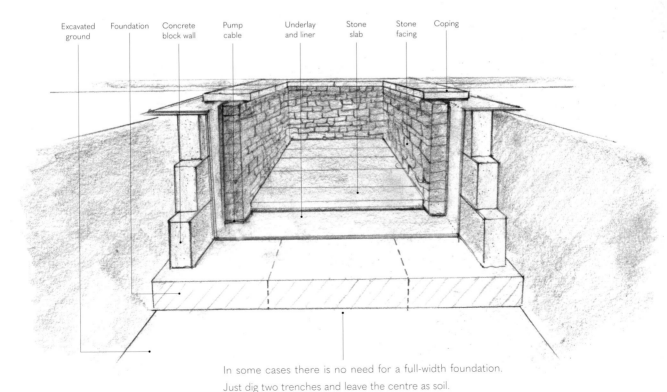

Excavated ground   Foundation   Concrete block wall   Pump cable   Underlay and liner   Stone slab   Stone facing   Coping

In some cases there is no need for a full-width foundation.
Just dig two trenches and leave the centre as soil.

"... Driving south we noticed a wall of sand through the trees.
A complete surprise that turned out to have a very memorable view ..."

" ... Harry holding his 9ft and Single, picking the right time to paddle out. Most of the time the waves aren't perfect, but the feeling of being out on the water – just you and the waves – operating in the present, is really special ..."

MOUNTAIN

"Whenever we drive back to Wales
we know the Brecons mean
ten minutes until we're home.
The unique sense of freedom
that this feeling creates is always
partnered with a humbling sense of
scale as the land towers over us."

Mountains possess a powerful atmosphere. Their challenging landscape requires our respect. Whenever we're walking mountain tracks we notice how exposed and harsh the conditions are, and how they control the palette of plants. Gnarled wind-blown trees and shrubs tell a story of strong. prevailing winds and undulating land, providing few sheltered spots away from the elements.

For us it's all about understanding the unique sense of place: looking at the natural materials, the way they weather, how roots are exposed on paths and how plants grow out of the most unlikely places.

MOUNTAIN ZONES

Mountain zones are the natural-layered ecosystems that occur at distinct altitudes due to a variety of environmental conditions. These include temperature, humidity, soil composition and solar radiation. As a result, the plant life in each zone is vastly different, from lush dense birch forests to gnarled pines and low-lying, waxy-leaved alpines.

NIVAL

Dominated by snow throughout the majority of the year. Vegetation is very limited.

ALPINE

BIOTEMPERATURE 1.5–3°C

Conditions are too harsh for trees to grow so this zone is dominated by a close carpet of grasses, sedges, cushion plants, mosses and lichens. These alpine plants have adapted to growing in intense radiation, wind, snow and ice.

TREELINE

The uppermost line at which trees are capable of growing. Beyond this they cannot survive in the unique environmental conditions, low temperature and lack of moisture.

KRUMHOLZ

This defines a type of stunted and deformed vegetation that is contorted and deformed by constant exposure to wind. It occurs when trees are at the absolute limit of their growing conditions.

SUB-ALPINE

BIOTEMPERATURE 3–6°C

Trees begin to thin out and can only grow in more sheltered spots. Their growth is limited. Meadows occur in this zone.

MONTANE

BIOTEMPERATURE 6–12°C

At moderate elevations the temperature and rainfall create the right conditions for the growth of dense forests.

FOOTHILLS

The lowest zone, defined as a gradual increase in elevation at the base of a mountain range. Foothill conditions vary depending on the surrounding landscape.

ELEMENT
TEXTURE

Mountains are steep and exposed. Stone paths, rocky outcrops and rugged vegetation outline a landscape that is wild and untamed.

Whenever we look to recreate a mountain-inspired landscape, texture is fundamental.

Exposed rock provides a harsh texture contrasting with softer invasive greenery

Stone is a very versatile material and can provide very different textures. In its natural state it can be coarse and jagged but when weathered and eroded over time it becomes smooth.

A smooth surface provides the illusion of a more trodden path, whereas a textured finish will make a more characterful impression.

It's the balance between rough and smooth that highlights the use of texture within the landscaping.

Some rock types are more resistant to weathering and therefore maintain a rugged surface quality

Smooth rock displays the effects of weathering over many years. This texture feels more inviting, and if used in a garden can make the space feel softer and more cosy. To recreate this texture, a process called bush hammering is used

PRINCIPLE
SPACE

The sheer scale of a mountain range provides a feeling of ultimate space. Whenever we walk the Brecon Beacons we pause often to appreciate the view shown here.

Being able to look down across a whole landscape is an awesome feeling and it's something that can be replicated in a garden by creating level changes.

Working with existing or creating level changes, whether large or small, can provide very different perspectives within a garden. The steeper north face of Cribyn accentuates the scale and height of the mountain whereas the opposite one slopes gradually down to the valley floor and seems less threatening.

Within your garden this same effect of contrasting gradients can be created by using either many low-level changes or fewer, larger level changes.

The mountain peak of Cribyn as seen from Pen-Y-Fan is one of our favourite views. The sheer expanse of steep mountain faces and rolling hills creates a great sense of enormity

INSPIRATION

Although not your typical picturesque mountain landscape, the raw bleakness portrayed in this photo held an honesty that was very inspiring to us.

The boldness of the rockfaces and the shadows created by the sun give this place real depth and mystery.

STONE-FACED
RETAINING WALL

CONCRETE STEPS

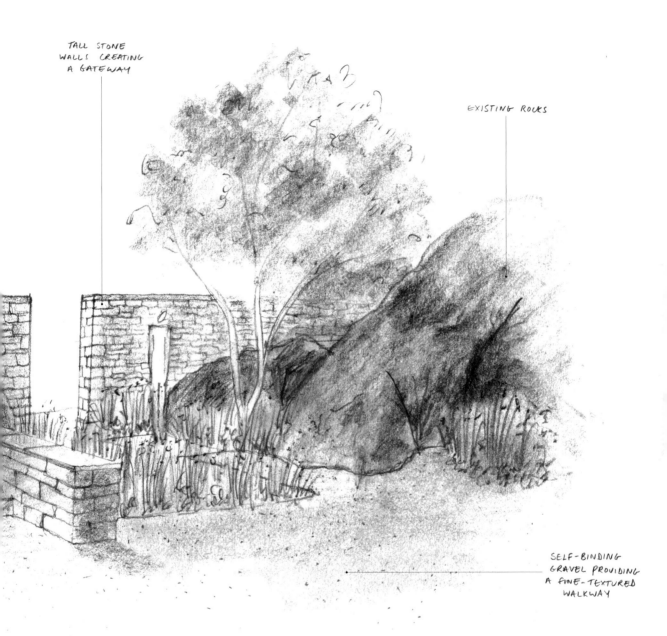

TALL STONE
WALLS CREATING
A GATEWAY

EXISTING ROCKS

SELF-BINDING
GRAVEL PROVIDING
A FINE-TEXTURED
WALKWAY

We wanted to design a space dominated by level changes and create the feeling of having to find your way down a rocky mountainside.

It was important to use stone to acknowledge the natural material but we wanted to contrast this texture with cast concrete steps, giving the impression of a smoother, more used surface.

The more distant path works around larger existing rocks that are softened with short, tough planting and shadowed by a multi-stemmed tree.

A high stone wall creates a gateway into another space, rewarding curiosity.

Isolating colours within a mountain habitat helps to inspire colour schemes within your garden. This Scottish landscape provides a vivid range of atmospheric colours that could be used to inspire the tones of stone stacked within a gabion or the dark needles of a gnarled pine.

DESIGN CONCEPTS

LEVEL CHANGES

Steps are an integral part of a garden. With careful thought about their function and aesthetics they can become stand-alone features. The sketches below demonstrate how variations in step design can dramatically alter the way a space is used, looks and feels.

UPPER TERRACE

Projecting steps out creates more space on the upper terrace.

LOWER TERRACE

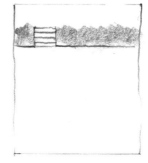

Setting steps back into the upper terrace creates more space on the lower terrace.

ALTERED DIRECTION

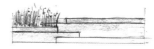

Altering the direction of steps causes you to journey away from the destination, briefly averting your attention.

MULTI-FUNCTION

USABLE
TERRACE

LOW
BENCH

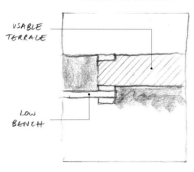

Enlarging the area of certain steps can create different finctions. From ground up.

HIDDEN

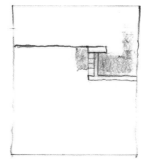

Concealing the steps within a dog-legged retaining wall completely hides them from view.

PLATFORM

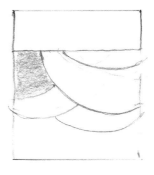

Platform steps provide a more gradual journey and their size creates a feature within the garden. Curving them evokes a more natural character.

Here the level change is controlled by a corten-steel divide. Its bold tone and architectural layout creates a prominent transition.

The burnt orange of the steel forms a deliberate connection with the wooden deck, creating a dialogue between the upper and lower terraces. The materials have been used to link two spaces that otherwise could have been seen as completely separate.

This bold retaining wall divides the land, creating a flat, open seating space. We wanted to accentuate this feature by continuing the steel further into the garden.

The solid form starts to open up into segmented panels, allowing light to filter through and opening views onto the extended landscape.

STEPS

The direction of steps can completely alter the character of a level change.

STRAIGHT

FOLDED

CURVED

ANGLED

This direct route creates a strong singular view.

Folding the steps creates multiple views as you travel up or down and a large landing to view the garden from.

Curving the steps allows your view to fan across the garden as you climb or descend the steps.

Angular steps also create multiple views as you use them, though provide a smaller landing space.

PLAN VIEW

Recessing steps parallel with the retaining wall is a great way of minimising the space they take up. It also creates a beautifully understated feature that gives the wall added depth and weight.

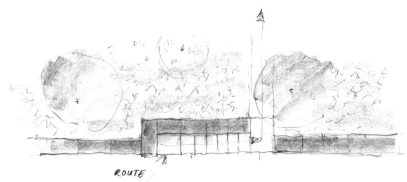

ROUTE

SECTION VISUAL

Using a thick cropped slab for the steps adds a real touch of quality and highlights the steps, contrasting with the stone walling.

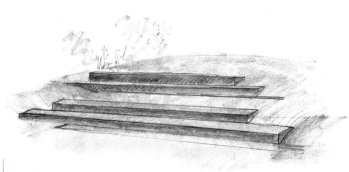

Isolated steps set within a sculpted bank can be a sympathetic way of dealing with a level change. The landform can blend around the steps, softening them into the landscape.

PATHS

When creating a path on a slope like this you would normally cut into the slope and only retain on the upper side.

But by sinking the path deeper into the slope retaining walls are needed on both sides. This creates a more intimate journey, mimicking a naturally weathered path formed by the elements, or the tracks of previous travellers, as your eye level is closer to the ground, providing you with a greater sense of connection to the land.

INSPIRED BY MOUNTAIN PEAKS

Introducing level changes into your garden can create a dramatic effect.

Triangular sheets of corten-steel joined at the peak, filled with soil and turfed/grass-seeded give the impression of grass protruding from the ground.

INSPIRED BY GLACIAL FORMS

A glacial cirque is an amphitheatre-shaped valley created by glacial erosion, cupped by the mountain but open on the downhill side.

We have adapted the concept of cupped valley sides into three separate designs, showing how simply adapting the levels can create such contrasting atmospheres.

A full-height retaining wall provides a very intimate space. A raised bench echoing the curve of the wall creates a cosy seat to look out from.

Continuing the retaining wall out at a single height completely encloses the platform.

To isolate the platform even more, you could remove the steps and close up the gap, making it only accessible from the top terrace.

Large semicircular steps retain soil to create a circular platform. The back wall retains the remaining soil to create a high seat.

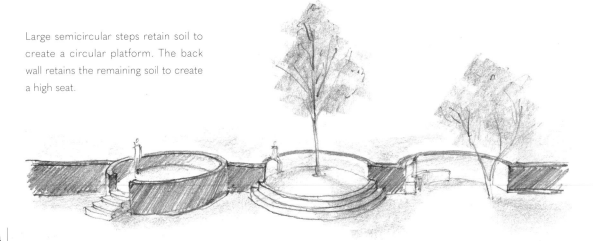

INSPIRED BY MAP CONTOURS

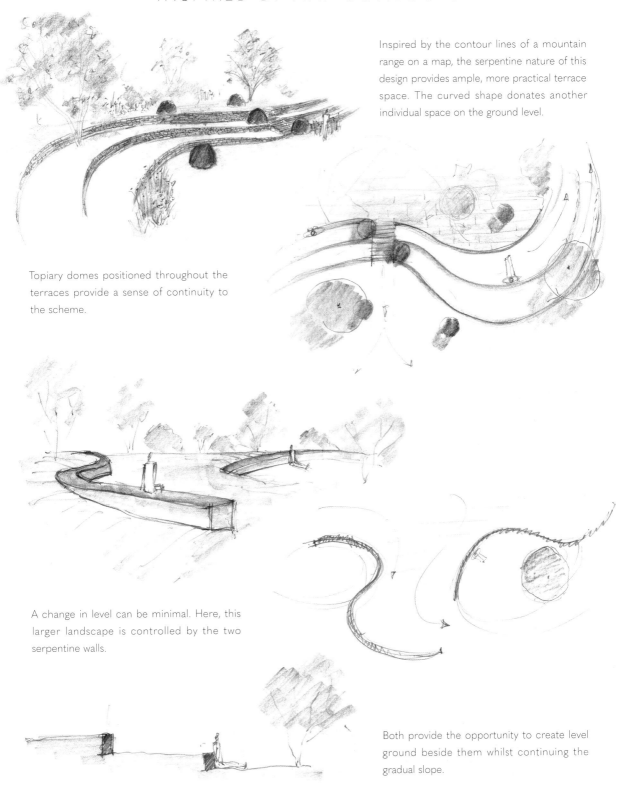

Inspired by the contour lines of a mountain range on a map, the serpentine nature of this design provides ample, more practical terrace space. The curved shape donates another individual space on the ground level.

Topiary domes positioned throughout the terraces provide a sense of continuity to the scheme.

A change in level can be minimal. Here, this larger landscape is controlled by the two serpentine walls.

Both provide the opportunity to create level ground beside them whilst continuing the gradual slope.

INSPIRED BY GROUND TEXTURES

When walking within a mountain habitat the ground beneath your feet is something that can easily be overlooked against the beauty and scale of the landscape. But when imitating this habitat within your garden it becomes a crucial design element.

NATURAL STONE

Using the same stone but in a variety of its natural forms will instantly lend an unrefined character. Recycling your old stone or sourcing it reclaimed is also a great way of adding character.

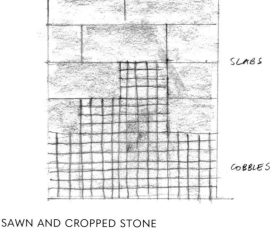

SAWN AND CROPPED STONE

Using the same stone in cut, geometric forms will provide a similar natural character but in a more modern style.

TEXTURED FINISHES

Using a slab with a manufactured finish can give a real sense of quality to the stone. This pattern is inspired by weathered layers of stone exposed on a mountain cliff. This is classed as a corduroy finish.

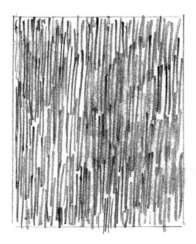

EDGE-LAID STONE

Laying thinly cropped stone creates a rougher, sharper texture that is more noticeable due to the irregular contours of the stone. Laying stone in this way also creates lots of pockets for mosses and plants to grow in.

These pages demonstrate a variety of ways in which you can use stone on the ground to replicate a mountain habitat, imitating weathered rocks, eroded paths and animal tracks.

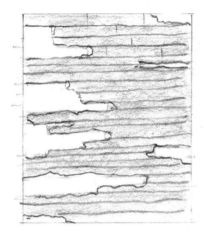

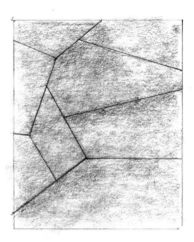

CONCRETE

Preformed slabs of concrete create a continuous floorscape with a cracked apperance. Designed well, it's a great way of replicating patterns found in nature but with a modern twist. The odd smaller slab could be left out to create a planting pocket.

BRICK

Brick is a very approachable material. Simply offsetting the edges creates a more fluid, unstructured character. Planting low-lying plants within the gaps softens the edges.

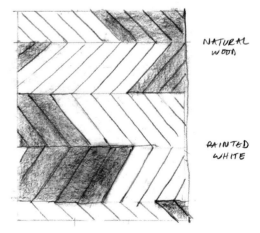

CORTEN-STEEL

Corten-steel strips are set within the lawn, allowing you to find your own route through the garden and resulting in a more focused, thoughtful journey.

WOOD

Herringbone decking with areas painted white. This can define a path or desired route across an expanse of deck.

A MOUNTAIN GARDEN

INITIAL CONCEPT

TOP LEVEL

Alpine meadow

Shrubs

Small area for seating to look
down over the garden

MID LEVEL

Open usable space

Transition through the levels

Possible lawn area

Water feature cascading down
levels

GROUND LEVEL

Functional space outside the
house

Area for dining, potentially
looking across water

Softened by planting

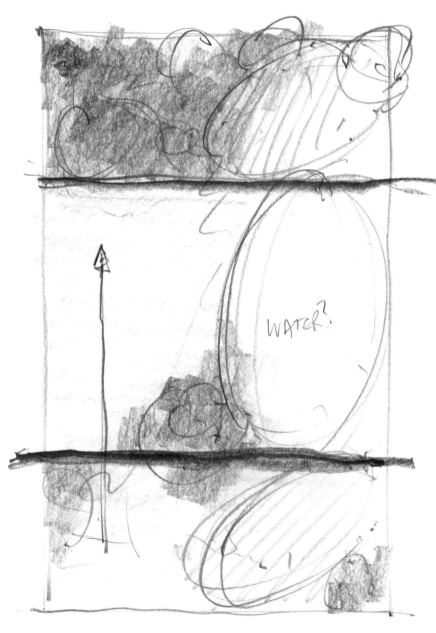

HOUSE

CONCEPT DEVELOPMENT

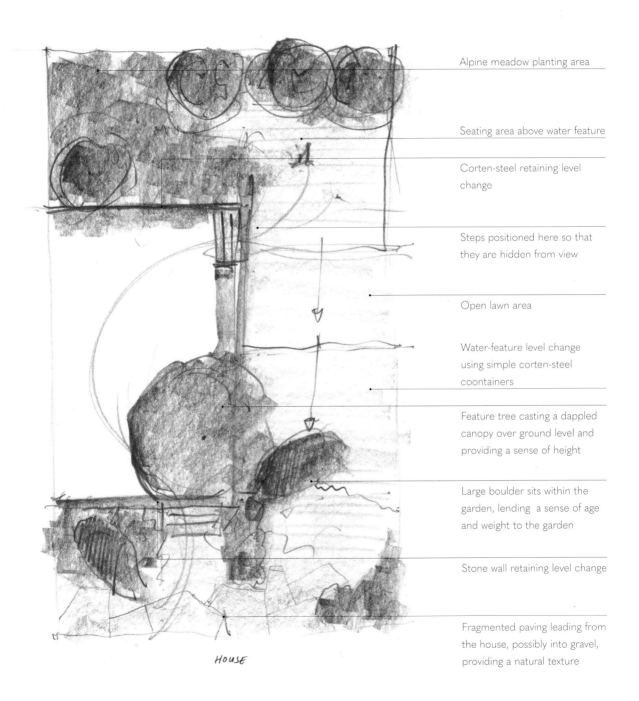

Alpine meadow planting area

Seating area above water feature

Corten-steel retaining level change

Steps positioned here so that they are hidden from view

Open lawn area

Water-feature level change using simple corten-steel coontainers

Feature tree casting a dappled canopy over ground level and providing a sense of height

Large boulder sits within the garden, lending a sense of age and weight to the garden

Stone wall retaining level change

Fragmented paving leading from the house, possibly into gravel, providing a natural texture

HOUSE

CONCEPT DEVELOPMENT

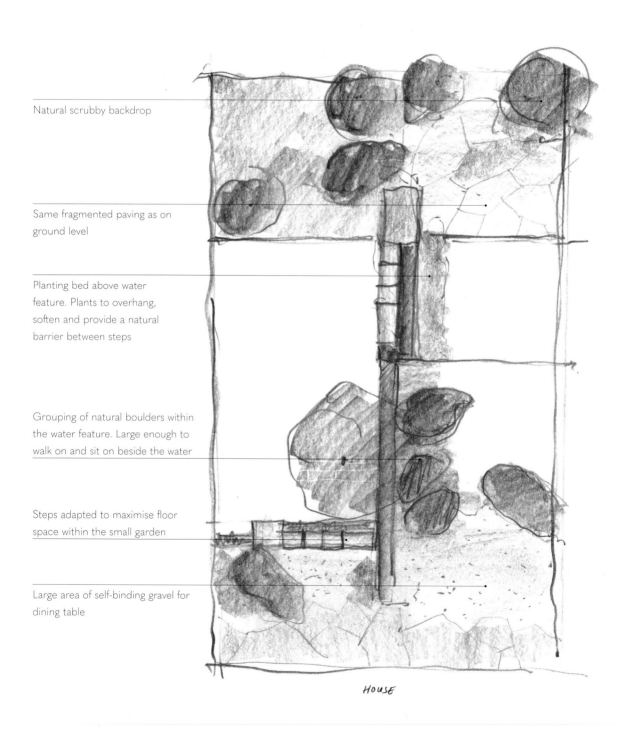

Natural scrubby backdrop

Same fragmented paving as on ground level

Planting bed above water feature. Plants to overhang, soften and provide a natural barrier between steps

Grouping of natural boulders within the water feature. Large enough to walk on and sit on beside the water

Steps adapted to maximise floor space within the small garden

Large area of self-binding gravel for dining table

HOUSE

FINAL DESIGN

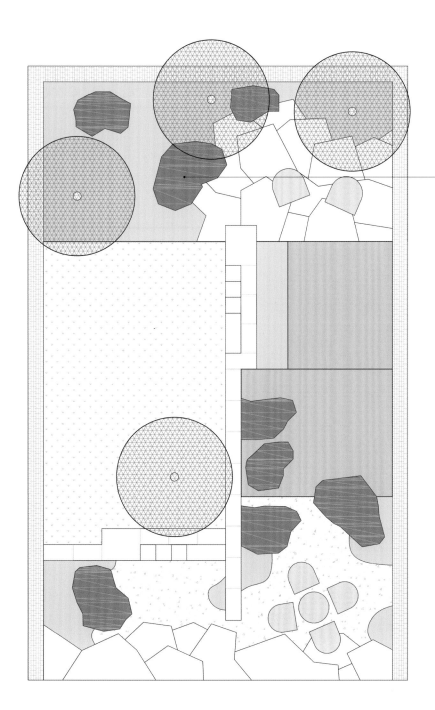

Only minor alterations were found to be necessary when finalising the design

Additional boulders to enhance the mountainous character of the garden

FINAL DESIGN VISUALS

This cross-section shows how creating three equally sized levels gives the garden a more gradual, less imposing perspective and provides three very distinct areas with separate uses.

This provides the impression of a more gentle mountain slope rather than a steeper rockface that would be achieved by using one full-height retaining wall.

The visual shows the view from the house. The angles of the fragmented paving stand out against the more minimal gravel and the strong forms of the stone walls cut through the garden. The design has a raw, slightly bare feeling to it but considered pockets of planting help to soften the harsher edges.

CONCEALED STEPS

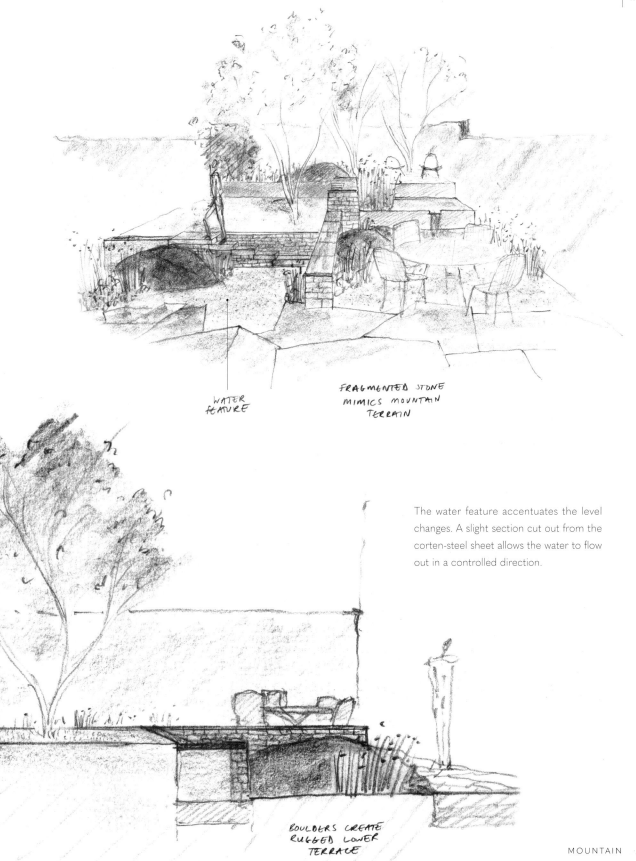

WATER
FEATURE

FRAGMENTED STONE
MIMICS MOUNTAIN
TERRAIN

The water feature accentuates the level
changes. A slight section cut out from the
corten-steel sheet allows the water to flow
out in a controlled direction.

BOULDERS CREATE
RUGGED LOWER
TERRACE

MOUNTAIN

MOUNTAIN PLANTING

High-altitude plants are, out of necessity, exceptionally hardy. The mountain landscape is barren, often rocky, providing few areas of shelter from the unrelenting wind.

When imitating a mountain habitat we take time to choose specific trees and shrubs with a more stunted, gnarled character, and position them as if they have been shaped by the wind.

Shorter, more woody shrubs like juniper or dwarf pine give the impression of plants surviving tough growing conditions, and low-lying planting imitates the vegetation that tightly hugs the undulating ground, only growing taller behind rocks and between cracks in the mountainside.

High-altitude alpine meadows are a carpet of green, rich in species diversity. But as the altitude increases the plants struggle to survive and rock becomes dominant. Snow and frost contour the mountainside for the majority of the year.

MOUNTAIN PLANTING SCHEME

INITIAL DESIGN PLAN

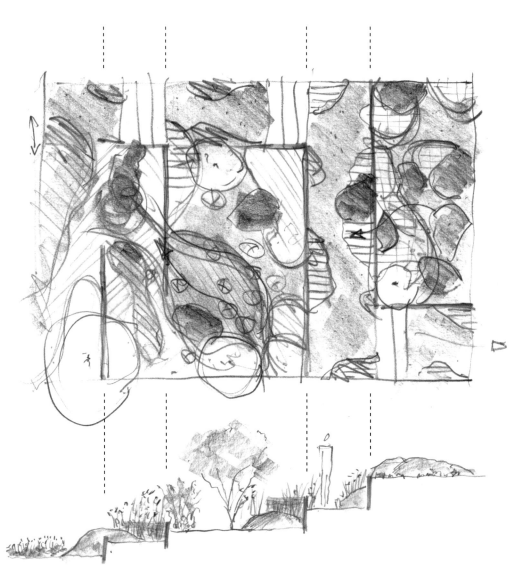

FOOTHILLS/MONTANE

Planting on the lower level is a lot more dense and full of foliage.

A tree represents the forests that grow in these zones.

SUB-ALPINE/ALPINE

Gravel from the path merges into the planting.

Planting starts to separate into individual clumps.

Low shrubs add character.

TRACK

Imitating a mountain track cut into the rock.

The gravel path is softened by pockets of perennials.

ALPINE/NIVAL

Plants surround the large rocks placed within the bed.

More stone and gravel visible.

Plants chosen for their low-growing habit.

DEVELOPED PLANTING PLAN

We wanted to demonstrate the concept of adapting plants across a scheme to imitate the individual zones found on a mountain.

This scheme fits into an area approx. 10×6m and has a change in level from top to bottom of approx. 1.5m.

We have adopted a modern approach to a traditional rock garden by using sheets of corten-steel to retain the soil, but still included rocks within the beds.

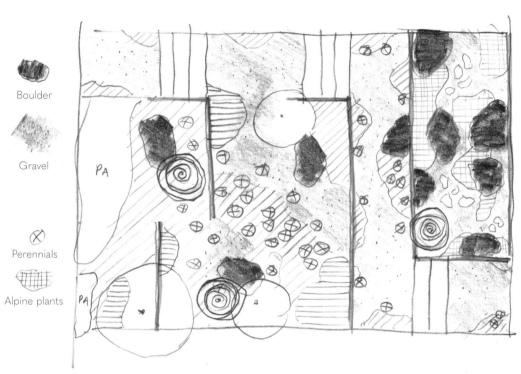

Boulder

Gravel

Perennials

Alpine plants

Persicaria

F. paniculata

F. glauca

Perovskia

Rhododendron

FOOTHILLS/MONTANE

Large drifts of

Knotweed
Persicaria affinis
'Darjeeling Red'

creates a green carpet with a thread of pink-crimson

Alpine violet fescue
Festuca paniculata

runs uphill.

A couple of

Dwarf purple rhododendron
Rhododendron impeditum

are placed next to boulders.

Scots pine
Pinus sylvestris

sits at the foothills of the slope.

SUB-ALPINE/ALPINE

Rugosa rose
Rosa rugosa

shrubs enclose the terrace where a central pocket of

Alpine violet fescue
Festuca paniculata

is interplanted with

Autumn sage
Salvia greggii
Catmint
Nepeta racemosa
'Walker's Low'

Large pockets of

Russian sage
Perovskia triplicifolia
'Blue Spire'

soften the corners.

TRACK

Alpine violet fescue
Festuca paniculata

softens the retaining corten-steel sheets

Autumn sage
Salvia greggii

forms individual clumps along the track.

ALPINE/NIVAL

Blue fescue
Festuca glauca
Dwarf hebe
Hebe buchananii 'Minor'
London pride
Saxifraga × urbium
Silvery yarrow
Achillea clavennae

form pockets around boulders.

Dwarf purple rhododendron
Rhododendron impeditum

clings to the edge of the terrace.

WIND/DROUGHT-TOLERANT
PERENNIALS

Autumn sage / Texas sage
Salvia greggii 'Lipstick'

A vibrant flower forming a clump of fresh green foliage that when touched releases a minty scent. It is a tender plant so will need winter protection but works really well in dry sunny spots. Looks good planted on its own in a pot, allowing it to fill out and spill over the sides. Bees, butterflies and moths love it.

HEIGHT ↕ 0.6m SPREAD ↔ 0.6m   FLOWERING ✳ JUN-OCT
POSITION ☼ FULL SUN   HARDINESS ❸ ④ ⑤ ⑥ ⑦

Granny's bonnet
Aquilegia vulgaris var. stellata 'Black Barlow'

Tough but beautiful plant with a distinctive divided leaf shape and pompom-like flowers. Its deep purple colour looks great with other darker flowering plants like Astrantia 'Ruby Star' and makes a stunning detail amongst grasses. Thrives in most conditions but grows best if the soil is kept moist over summer.

HEIGHT ↕ 0.9m SPREAD ↔ 0.45m   FLOWERING ✳ MAY-JUN
POSITION ☼ FULL SUN ❄ PARTIAL SHADE HARDINESS ③ ④ ⑤ ⑥ ❼

Japanese anemone
Anemone × hybrida 'Honorine Jobert'

Perfect for brightening up a shady area. Tall elegant plant with strong wiry stems and a clump of dark green semi-evergreen foliage. Grows in all soil types, provided they drain well.

HEIGHT ↕ 1.2m SPREAD ↔ 1.2m   FLOWERING ✳ AUG-OCT
POSITION ☼ FULL SUN ❄ PARTIAL SHADE HARDINESS ② ④ ⑤ ⑥ ❼

Beardtongue
Penstemon 'Raven'

A semi-evergreen perennial forming a clump of stiff stems, narrow leaves and bell-shaped flowers. Really easy to grow and will quickly bulk up. Prefers a sunny spot and lighter, well-drained soil.

HEIGHT ↕ 1m SPREAD ↔ 0.3m   FLOWERING ✳ JUN-OCT
POSITION ☼ FULL SUN ❄ PARTIAL SHADE HARDINESS ❸ ④ ⑤ ⑥ ⑦

❸ hardy in coastal and relatively mild parts of the UK [-5 to 1°C]   ❹ hardy through most of the UK [-10 to -5°C]
❺ hardy in most places throughout the UK, even in severe winters [-15 to -10°C] ❻ hardy in all of UK and northern Europe [-20 to -15°C]
❼ hardy in the severest European continental climates [-20°C and lower]

Lambs' ears

Stachys byzantina 'Silver Carpet'

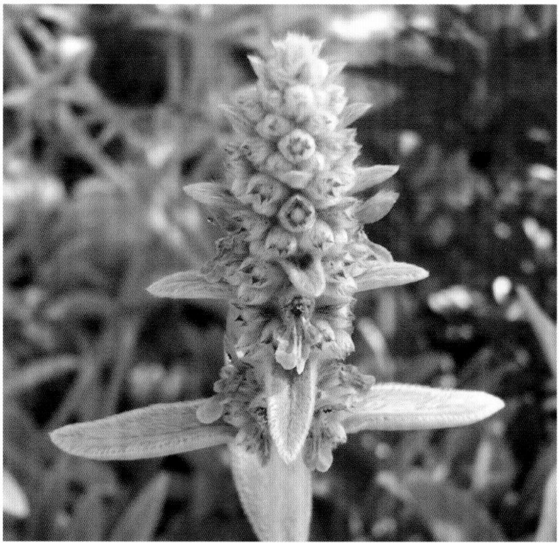

As the name suggests it is a great plant for creating a carpet-like effect with its evergreen foliage. Grows well in lighter, well-drained soils.

HEIGHT ↕ 0.2m SPREAD ↔ 0.45m FLOWERING ✻ JUN-AUG

POSITION ☼ FULL SUN HARDINESS 3 4 5 6 **7**

Wormwood

Artemisia 'Powis Castle'

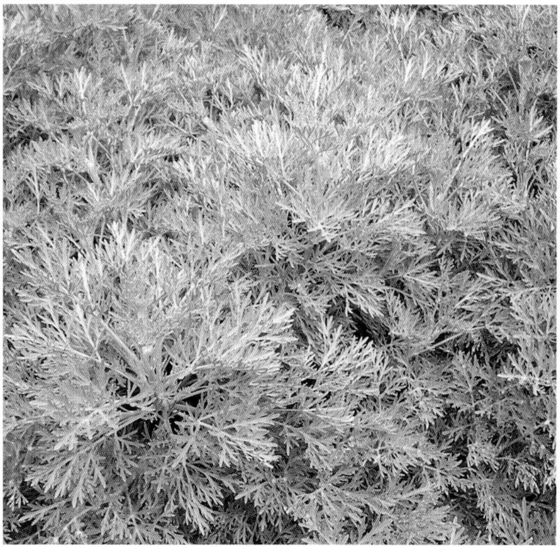

An evergreen dwarf shrub with a round bushy habit. Fine silvery aromatic leaves are the best part of this plant though it does produce a dull yellow flower. Increases its life if in a well-drained spot. Grows in chalk, sand and loam.

HEIGHT ↕ 0.6m SPREAD ↔ 0.9m FLOWERING ✻ AUG

POSITION ☼ FULL SUN HARDINESS **3** 4 5 6 7

Catmint

Nepeta 'Six Hills Giant'

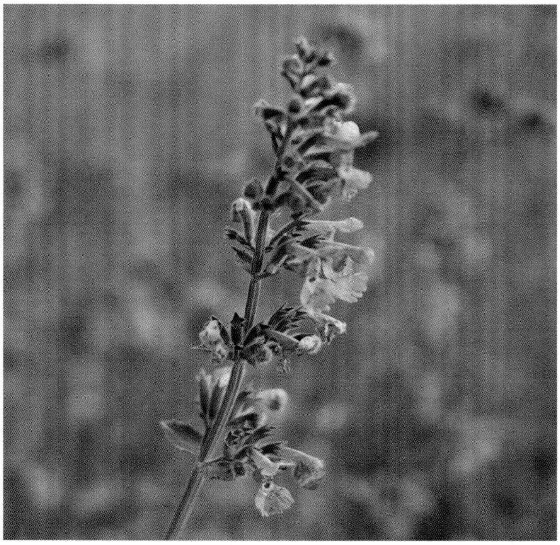

A vigorous growing bushy perennial with aromatic grey-green deciduous leaves and dusty purple flowers. Tolerates all soil types but prefers it well drained. A tough plant that can tolerate some shade throughout the day. Bees are highly attracted to the flowers and cats to the foliage: place sticks in the clump to prevent them flattening it.

HEIGHT ↕ 0.9m SPREAD ↔ 0.6m FLOWERING ✻ JUN-JUL

POSITION ☼ FULL SUN HARDINESS 3 4 5 6 **7**

Russian sage

Perovskia atriplicifolia 'Blue Spire'

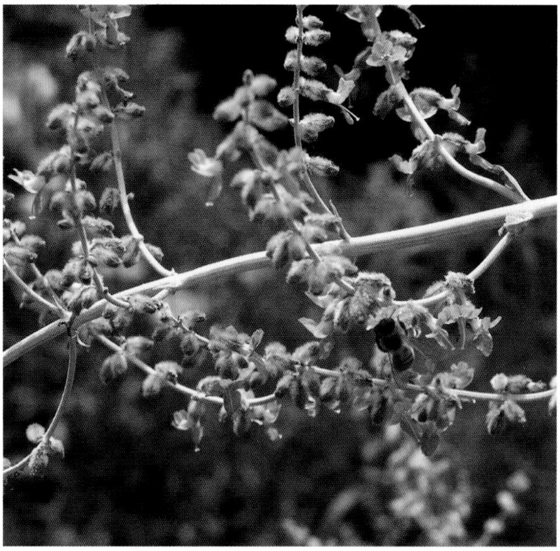

Perovskia is actually a dwarf shrub. With its aromatic leaves and strong architectural form it looks great amongst other late-flowering plants such as rudbeckia and Japanese anemone.

HEIGHT ↕ 1.2m SPREAD ↔ 1m FLOWERING ✻ AUG-SEP

POSITION ☼ FULL SUN HARDINESS 3 4 **5** 6 7

WIND/DROUGHT-TOLERANT

GRASSES

Mexican feather grass
Stipa tenuissima

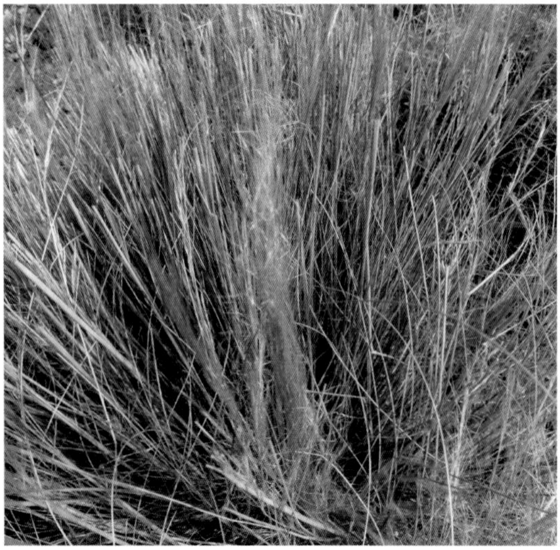

A deciduous tufted grass that produces wispy leaves and soft plumes of silvery-green flowers. Grows well in all soil types as long as they are free-draining. Provides stunning movement within a planting bed.

HEIGHT ↕ 0.6m SPREAD ↔ 0.3m FLOWERING ❋ JUN–SEP
POSITION ☼ FULL SUN HARDINESS 3 **4** 5 6 7

New Zealand blue grass
Poa labillardierei

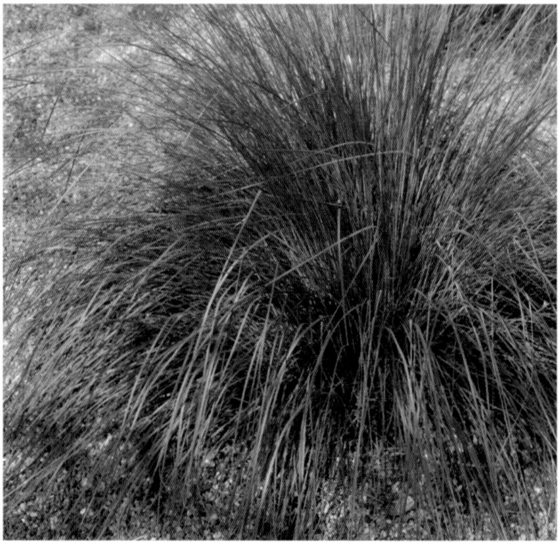

A semi-evergreen grass forming a dense clump of steel-blue narrow leaves and a purple flower in midsummer. Less tolerant of wind but is great for a dry spot in the garden. Prefers a mid to light soil that is well drained.

HEIGHT ↕ 1.2m SPREAD ↔ 0.8m FLOWERING ❋ JUN–AUG
POSITION ☼ FULL SUN HARDINESS 3 **4** 5 6 7

Alpine violet fescue
Festuca paniculata

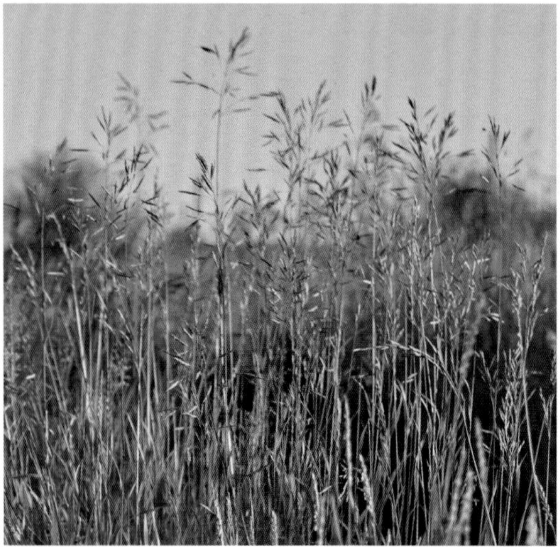

This grass produces dense clumps of flat evergreen leaves and displays delicate violet-tinged flowers in early summer. Grows best in a sunny spot with light, well-drained soil. .

HEIGHT ↕ 0.8m SPREAD ↔ 0.3m FLOWERING ❋ MAY–JUN
POSITION ☼ FULL SUN ☼ PARTIAL SHADE HARDINESS 3 4 5 **6** 7

Chinese silver grass 'Morning Light'
Miscanthus sinensis 'Morning Light'

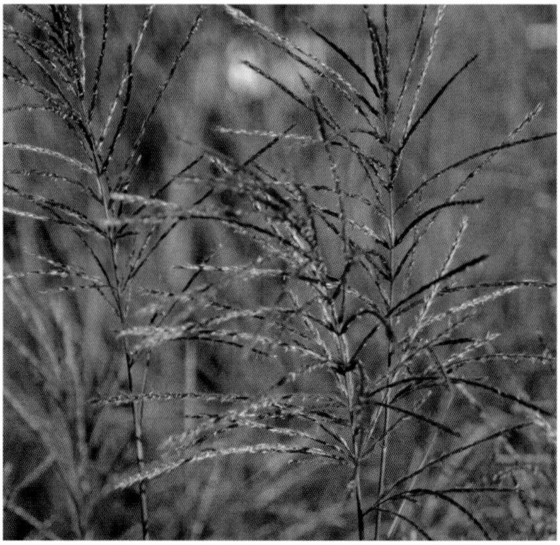

A compact deciduous grass with fine-edged upright leaves. This is not invasive so easy to control within a garden. Grows in all soil types provided they are moist but well drained. If it's a good year for sun the flowers will appear pinkish-brown.

HEIGHT ↕ 1.2m SPREAD ↔ 1.2m FLOWERING ❋ OCT–NOV
POSITION ☼ FULL SUN HARDINESS 3 4 5 **6** 7

Leatherleaf sedge

Carex buchananii 'Red Rooster'

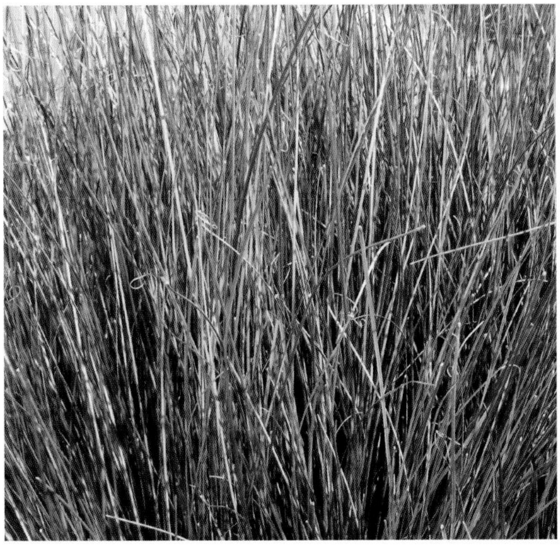

A unique grass with a copper/sepia tone. Really stiff and architectural with curled tops. It produces a dense clump of evergreen leaves that bear a brown spiked flower. Thrives in a well-drained soil and is easy to look after.

HEIGHT ↕ 0.6m SPREAD ↔ 0.5m FLOWERING ❋ JUN

POSITION ☀ FULL SUN ◐ PARTIAL SHADE HARDINESS 3 **4** 5 6 7

Oriental fountain grass

Pennisetum orientale

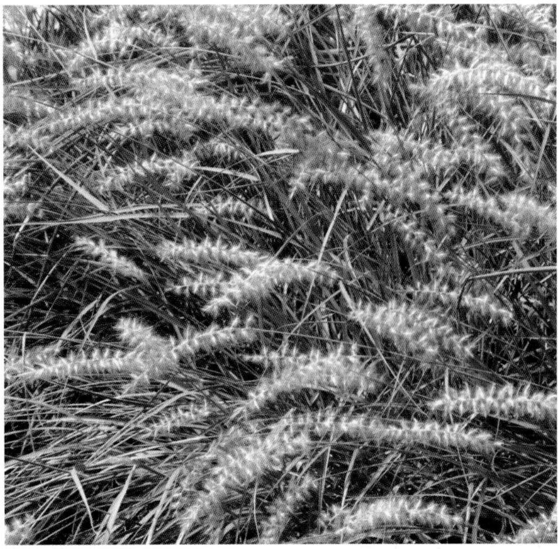

Dense, rounded clumps of narrow arching leaves topped with fuzzy, copper-pink flower spikes. Works well as a filler between perennials and used en masse. A very carefree plant that grows best in full sun and well-drained soil.

HEIGHT ↕ 0.8m SPREAD ↔ 0.6m FLOWERING ❋ JUL-SEP

POSITION ☀ FULL SUN ◐ PARTIAL SHADE HARDINESS 3 4 **5** 6 7

Berkeley sedge

Carex divulsa

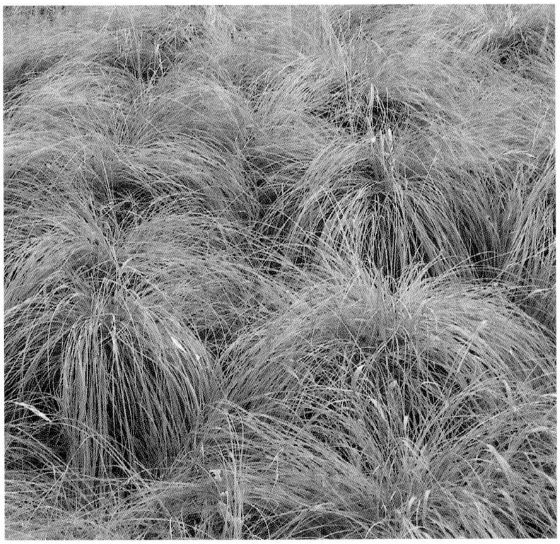

A low-lying clump-forming grass that produces drooping mounds of dark green evergreen foliage. It's perfect for creating a carpet effect en masse. Can tolerate most soil types, dry or damp and sun or shade. Found naturally along streams in northern California it combines nicely with ferns such as Polystichum *and perennials such as* Heuchera*. Extremely tough once established.*

HEIGHT ↕ 0.4m SPREAD ↔ 0.6m FLOWERING ❋ JUN-AUG

POSITION ☀ FULL SUN ◐ PARTIAL SHADE HARDINESS 3 **4** 5 6 7

Chinese silver grass 'Kleine Silberspinne's

Miscanthus 'Kleine Silberspinne'

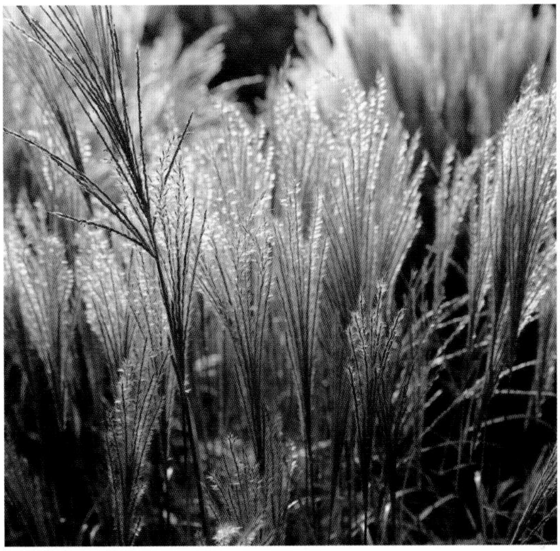

A tall eye-catching grass that doesn't take up too much space. Elegant fine foliage forms a distinct compact mound with silky silver-red flowers. This grass looks stunning in winter. Grows in all soils provided they are moist but well drained.

HEIGHT ↕ 1.2m SPREAD ↔ 0.45m FLOWERING ❋ SEP-OCT

POSITION ☀ FULL SUN HARDINESS 3 4 5 **6** 7

PLANTING MIX

Gardens can be controlled by many of the same environmental conditions as a mountain habitat. They can be prone to drought and colder temperatures and have to withstand exposure to wind. This meadow mix provides the individual species that will thrive in such conditions.

PRIMARY SPECIES <70%

↑ **Common sorrel**
Rumex acetosa

Sheep's fescue
Festuca ovina

Slender creeping red fescue
Festuca rubra litoralis

SECONDARY SPECIES <20%

↑ **Heather**
Calluna vulgaris

Sweet vernal grass
Anthoxanthum odoratum

Tall oat grass
Arrhenatherum elatius

Foxglove
Digitalis purpurea

Tufted hair grass
Deschampsia cespitosa

Wavy hair grass
Deschampsia flexuosa

TERTIARY SPECIES <10%

↑ **Primrose**
Primula vulgaris

Heath bedstraw
Galium saxatile

Pignut
Conopodium majus

Devil's bit scabious
Succisa pratensis

Tormentil
Potentilla erecta

EVERGREEN

ALPINES

Dwarf purple rhododendron

Rhododendron impeditum

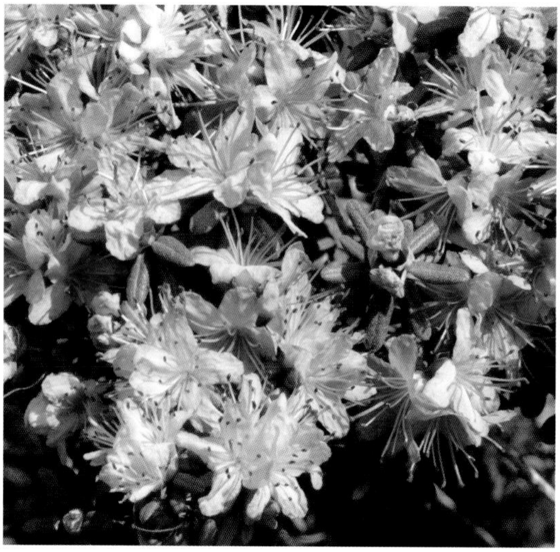

This dwarf rhododendron has small evergreen leaves with a soft scent. A compact low mound produces bold purple-blue flowers. Grows in acid soil and prefers it moist and well drained. Avoid planting too deeply.

HEIGHT ↕ 0.6m SPREAD ↔ 0.6m FLOWERING ✻ APR-MAY
POSITION ☀ FULL SUN ◐ PARTIAL SHADE HARDINESS 3 4 5 **6** 7

Candytuft

Iberis sempervirens

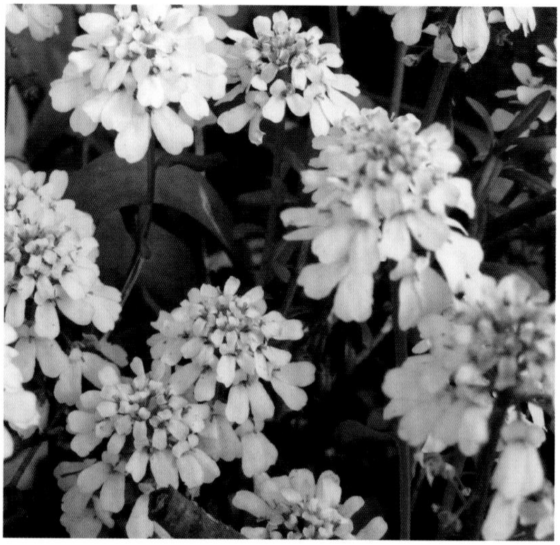

A spreading evergreen dwarf shrub with narrow dark green leaves. A trouble-free groundcover plant that makes a perfect green backdrop for other alpines like thrift and early dwarf bulbs. Plant on the edge of paths to soften the boundary between hard and soft. Grows best in a light, well-drained soil.

HEIGHT ↕ 0.3m SPREAD ↔ 0.4m FLOWERING ✻ APR-MAY
POSITION ☀ FULL SUN HARDINESS 3 4 **5** 6 7

Dwarf hebe

Hebe buchananii 'Minor'

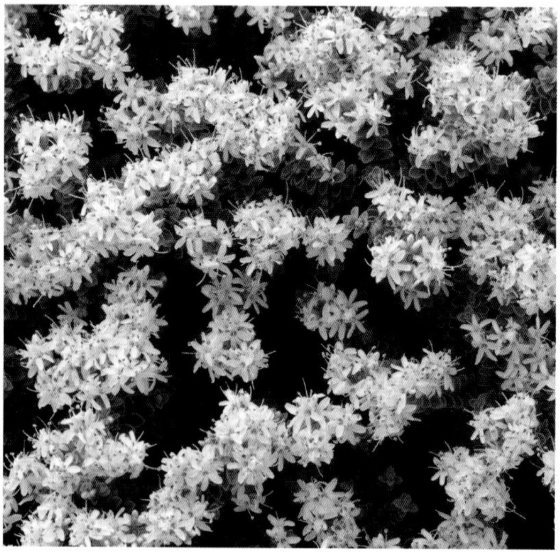

A small slow-growing hebe that forms low clumps of tiny evergreen leaves. A spreading plant with delicate white flowers in summer. Grows in most soil types provided they are free-draining. Prefers a pH that is neutral or alkaline.

HEIGHT ↕ 0.1m SPREAD ↔ 0.15m FLOWERING ✻ MAY-JUN
POSITION ☀ FULL SUN ◐ PARTIAL SHADE HARDINESS 3 **4** 5 6 7

London pride

Saxifraga × urbium

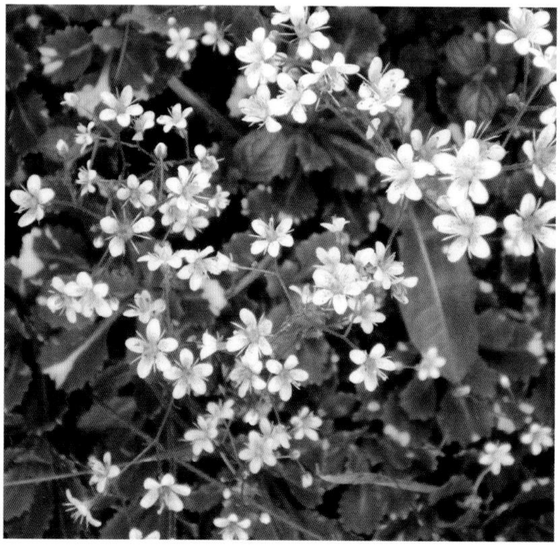

London Pride is an evergreen mat-forming perennial. Produces a delicate flower on a slender stem. Grows in all well-drained soil types.

HEIGHT ↕ 0.3m SPREAD ↔ 0.2m FLOWERING ✻ APR-JUN
POSITION ◐ PARTIAL SHADE ☼ SHADE HARDINESS 3 4 **5** 6 7

Silvery yarrow

Achillea clavennae

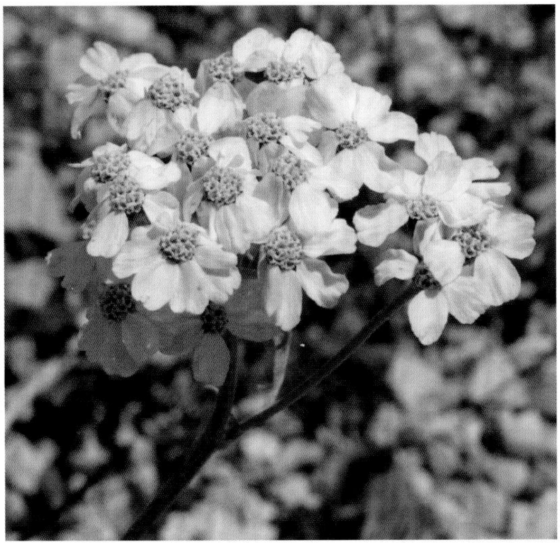

Grey-green fern-like leaves spread out to form an ideal groundcover. This heat and drought-tolerant perennial can become invasive due to its fibrous root system, but as long as you divide annually it can be contained. Great for bees and butterflies.

HEIGHT ↕ 0.2m SPREAD ↔ 0.3m FLOWERING JUN–AUG
POSITION ☼ FULL SUN HARDINESS 3 4 5 [6] 7

Knotweed

Persicaria affinis 'Darjeeling Red'

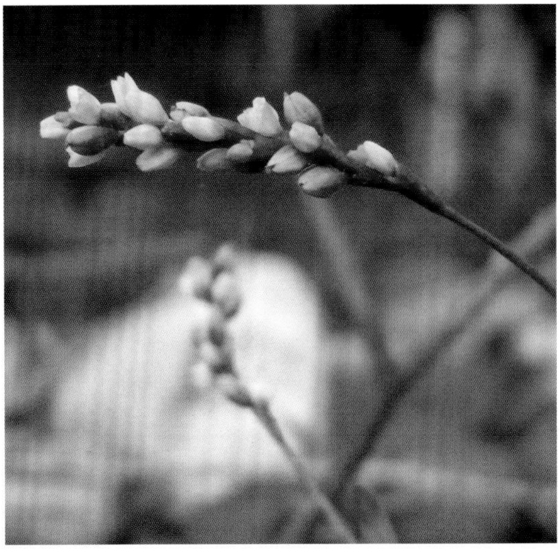

This is a semi-evergreen perennial that forms a mat of lance-shaped leaves. It makes excellent groundcover on banks or on walls. Tolerant of very dry conditions. Spikes of small white flowers become darker red when mature. Tolerates all poor-quality soils, moist or well drained.

HEIGHT ↕ 0.3m SPREAD ↔ 0.6m FLOWERING JUL–OCT
POSITION ☼ FULL SUN ◐ PARTIAL SHADE HARDINESS 3 4 5 [6] 7

Pine-leaved penstemon

Penstemon pinifolius

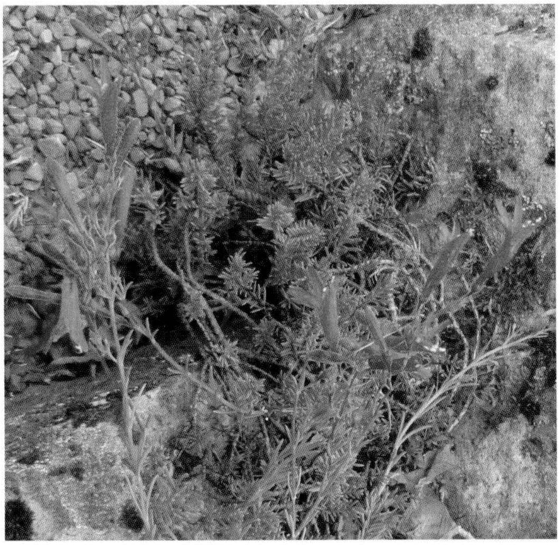

A species native to south-west America. This evergreen dwarf shrub forms a low bushy mound of needle-like leaves. Looks great in a rock garden and grows best in a sandy soil.

HEIGHT ↕ 0.3m SPREAD ↔ 0.4m FLOWERING JUN–AUG
POSITION ☼ FULL SUN HARDINESS 3 [4] 5 6 7

White flax

Linum suffruticosum

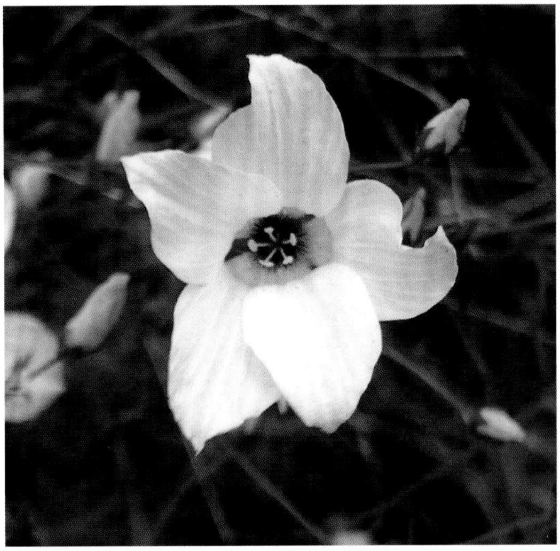

A woody-based perennial with a round bushy growth habit. Grows in light poor soils and open stony areas.

HEIGHT ↕ 0.15m SPREAD ↔ 0.3m FLOWERING JUL–AUG
POSITION ☼ FULL SUN ◐ PARTIAL SHADE HARDINESS 3 [4] 5 6 7

WIND/DROUGHT-TOLERANT

SHRUBS

Arrowwood viburnum

Viburnum dentatum

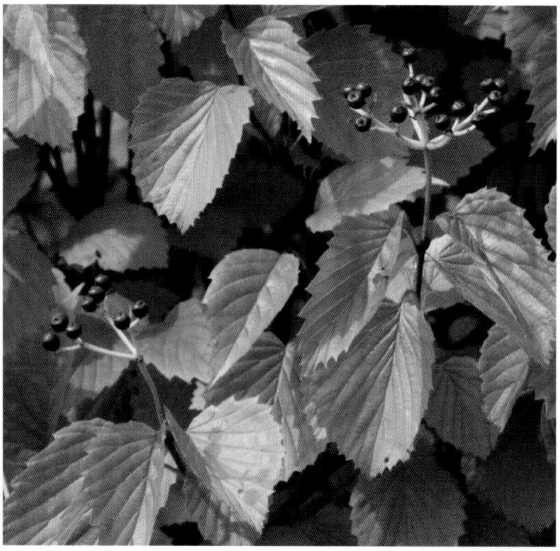

Native to North America, this dense deciduous multi-stemmed shrub has an overall oval shape. It's very easy to grow and highly adaptable so can tolerate varied conditions but prefers a sunny spot. Looks best in mass groupings. Has a simple flat dark green leaf and blue-black fruits.

HEIGHT ↕ 2m SPREAD ↔ 2m FLOWERING MAY–JUN
POSITION FULL SUN PARTIAL SHADE HARDINESS 3 4 **5** 6 7

Blackthorn

Prunus spinosa

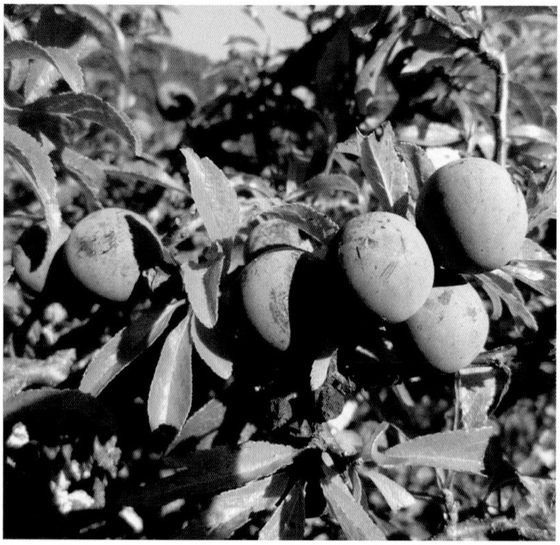

A large deciduous shrub/small tree with spiny and dense branches. Smooth dark brown bark and wrinkled oval pointed leaves. White flowers appear on short stalks before the leaves in March. For pollinators it's a great source of early nectar. Grows in all soils that are moist but well drained.

HEIGHT ↕ 4m SPREAD ↔ 4m FLOWERING MAR–APR
POSITION FULL SUN HARDINESS 3 4 5 6 **7**

Rugosa rose

Rosa rugosa

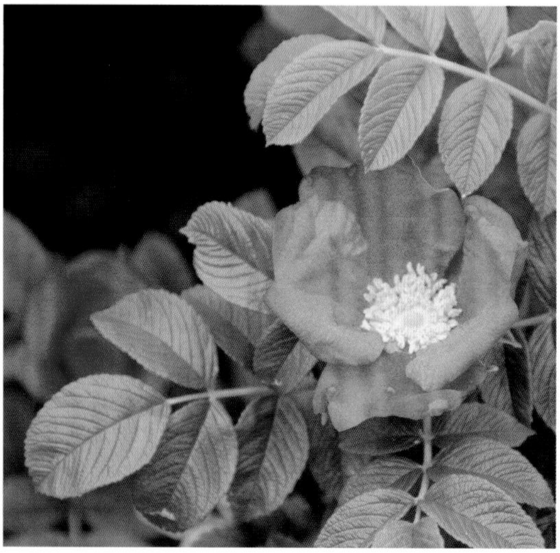

Native to the wind-blasted dunes of Russia and Japan this is naturally very tough. It's a perfect informal choice for a wild part of the garden. Produces a beautiful purple-red flower with leathery dark green leaves that turn gold in autumn. A fast-growing shrub that grows best in fertile, moist but well-drained soil.

HEIGHT ↕ 1.5m SPREAD ↔ 1.5m FLOWERING JUL–SEP
POSITION FULL SUN HARDINESS 3 4 5 **6** 7

Purple osier

Salix purpurea

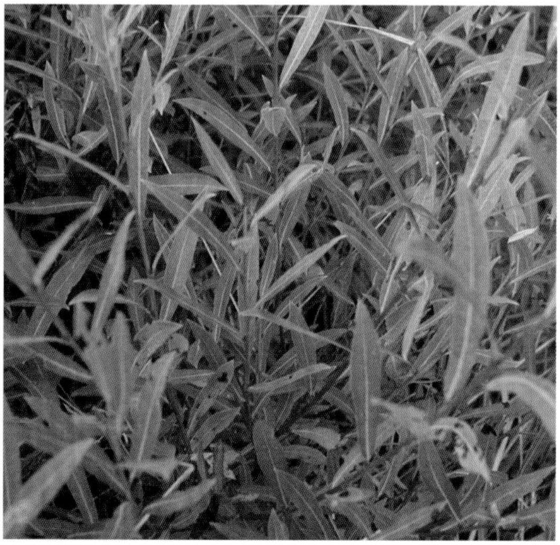

Not drought-tolerant but is perfect for wetter soils in exposed sites. An attractive, fast-growing native deciduous shrub with a spreading bushy habit. Year-round interest is achieved through red-purple arching stems. Great for stabilising wet waterside banks.

HEIGHT ↕ 6m SPREAD ↔ 4m FLOWERING MAR–APR
POSITION FULL SUN HARDINESS 3 4 5 **6** 7

White poplar

Poplus alba

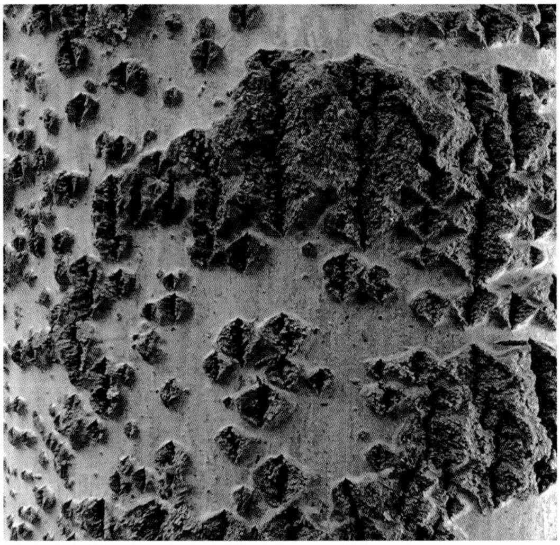

Not drought-tolerant but great for a windy spot. A medium-sized, fast-growing deciduous suckering tree that does well in moist soils. Its large leaves make this an attractive sight and it supports a range of insects, butterflies and moths.

HEIGHT ↕ 15m SPREAD ↔ 8m+ FLOWERING ✻ MAR
POSITION ☼ FULL SUN HARDINESS ❸ 4 5 6 7

Serviceberry

Amelanchier canadensis

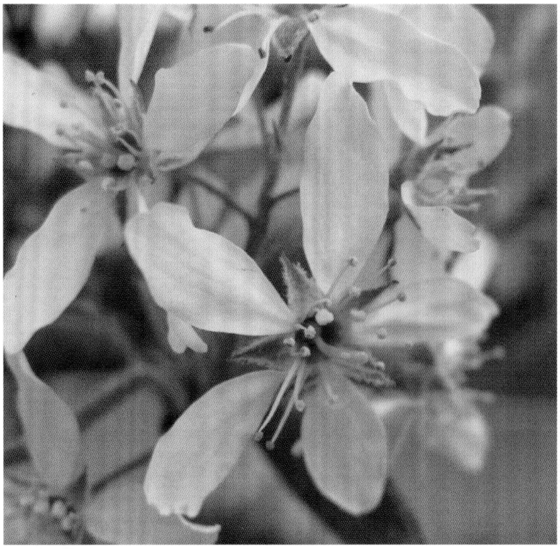

A good tree for an exposed smaller garden, drought-tolerant when mature. Usually grown as a multi-stem, it has real sculptural stature. Its leaves mature to a dark green, turning orange-red in autumn. Beautiful spring blossom and an edible fruit in summer. Doesn't grow in chalk, preferring a moist, well-drained soil.

HEIGHT ↕ 10m SPREAD ↔ 12m FLOWERING ✻ MAR-APR
POSITION ☼ FULL SUN ◐ PARTIAL SHADE HARDINESS 3 4 5 6 ❼

Scots pine

Pinus sylvestris

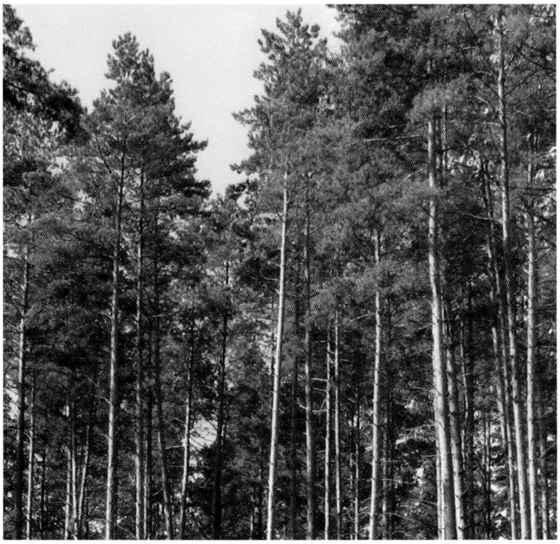

A large evergreen with slightly twisted, blue-green needle-like leaves. After pollination the female flowers develop into cones. The upper trunk and branches are orange-brown, developing an irregular shape with maturity. Tolerates all soil types and grows best in well-drained soil.

HEIGHT ↕ 20m SPREAD ↔ 8+m FLOWERING ✻ APR
POSITION ☼ FULL SUN HARDINESS 3 4 5 6 ❼

Rowan / Mountain ash

Sorbus aucuparia

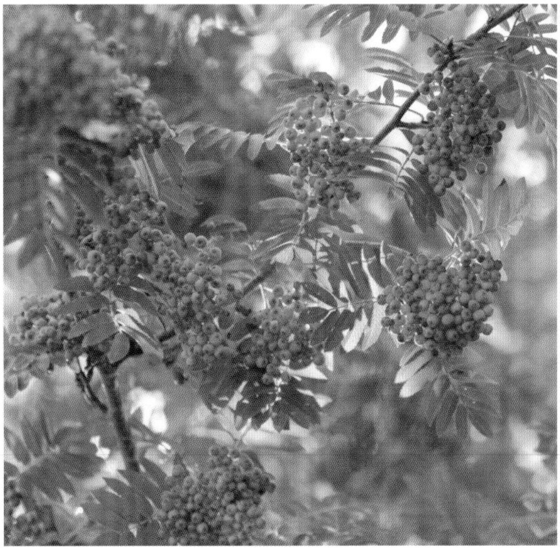

A native species that is found everywhere at home in Wales. Small upright deciduous tree with simple pinnate leaves that flowers in early summer and produces vivid berries in early autumn. Grows into a conical shape and can tolerate very harsh conditions. Requires a loam or sand soil that is well drained.

HEIGHT ↕ 8m SPREAD ↔ 5m+ FLOWERING ✻ MAY-JUN
POSITION ☼ FULL SUN ◐ PARTIAL SHADE HARDINESS 3 4 5 ❻ 7

CONSTRUCTING RETAINING WALLS

WHY

Level changes can indicate a transition from one individual space to another, they can be pronounced or understated but the key, as ever, is in the detail. A level change provides a different perspective on the garden: as you step up it offers an extended view, whilst as you drop down you get a more enclosed, intimate impression.

There are many different ways of dealing with level changes. These can be natural and sympathetic, like a gentle sloping lawn between some trees, or they can be more structural, like a retaining dry-stone wall that tucks back into the landscape. Level changes should be pivotal within the garden. They should be considered and sit effortlessly within the surrounding design.

GABION RETAINING WALLS

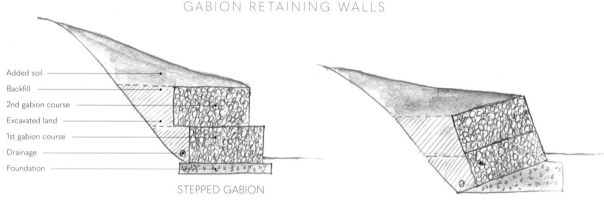

Added soil
Backfill
2nd gabion course
Excavated land
1st gabion course
Drainage
Foundation

STEPPED GABION

TILTED GABION

HOW

1: Excavate the land away from final gabion position. The bank should be excavated at a stable angle.

2: If the soil is compacted a low gabion wall will not require a foundation because of its weight.

To create a tilted gabion the foundation needs to be created on an angle.

3: Place the first gabion course in position and lace together with tie wire before filling with chosen material.

4: Backfill and compact to top of cage. Poor compaction could lead to lateral wall movement and damage to the wall. Stone and gravel are a perfect backfill material.

Depending on the permeability of the chosen material within the gabion cage you may need to add drainage.

5: Position second gabion course set back from first for stability, lace together all connecting cages. Fill cage and backfill to top of cage.

6: Landscape bank over the top gabion to provide a more sympathetic look.

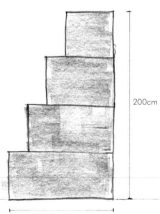

200cm

130cm

NOTE

When constructing a large retaining wall there is a simple rule to make sure it is strong enough to take the weight of what it is retaining.

The width at the base of the wall should be approximately two-thirds the height of the wall.

TRADITIONAL STONE RETAINING WALL

HOW

1: Excavate the bank ready for the wall's foundation.

Traditionally field walls didn't have foundations but using crushed stone or concrete provides a more stable base for the wall.

2: Place a drainage pipe behind the wall. This prevents any water build-up and additional pressure.

3: Larger, weightier foundation stones make up the majority of the lower wall. Infilling the void space with smaller stone is fundamental to keeping the wall rigid. Backfill with small angular pieces as you progress so that the wall is always stable and free-draining.

4: As you continue constructing the wall the use of through stones is critical to create strength.

5: The wall should have a tapered apperance to ensure that it can withstand the weight load from the bank.

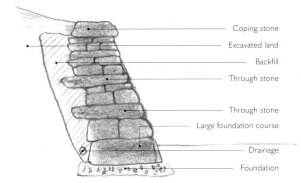

Coping stone
Excavated land
Backfill
Through stone
Through stone
Large foundation course
Drainage
Foundation

6: As you move towards the desired height ensure the tapered angle continues and finish with a large coping stone.

7: Landscape the bank.

BLOCK AND SINGLE-FACED RETAINING WALL

HOW

1: Excavate the bank ready for the wall's foundation.

2: Create a concrete footing to form a solid base for the wall and place drainage pipe behind.

3: Lay the concrete blocks to the desired height to create a strong retaining wall. Wait until this goes off.

4: Using cropped 8in walling stone, start to face the concrete blocks, adding mortar in the gaps between the block and the stone.

To create a more authentic character avoid using mortar to bed the stone.

Continue constructing in this method. Allow mortar to go off before continuing too high so that the wall doesn't become weak and damaged.

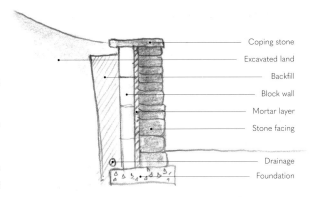

Coping stone
Excavated land
Backfill
Block wall
Mortar layer
Stone facing
Drainage
Foundation

5: When you reach the desired height, finish with a coping stone to conceal the concrete block.

6: Fill the cavity behind the concrete block with drainage stone.

7: Landscape bank into wall.

CONSTRUCTING STEPS

STONE-EDGED STEPS

WHY

There are many different styles of steps available but the advantage offered by a flight of edged steps is that it is possible to create a permeable surface behind the edge, preventing water from rushing down onto the area below.

HOW

1: Excavate the ground, clearly defining the shapes of the steps.

2: Lay a granular sub-base to form a solid footing to construct the steps on. This also helps to protect from frost.

3: Set the large paving stones into a mortar strip foundation.

Haunch the top corners so that the strip foundation doesn't infringe on the paving.

Make sure the final levels of the large paving stones are correct.

4: Infill with a granular load-bearing course.

5: Finally, place chosen paving onto a shallow mortar base.

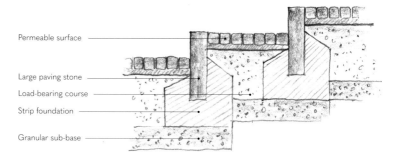

Permeable surface
Large paving stone
Load-bearing course
Strip foundation
Granular sub-base

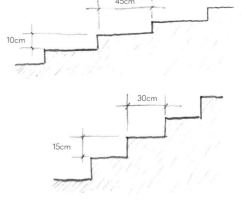

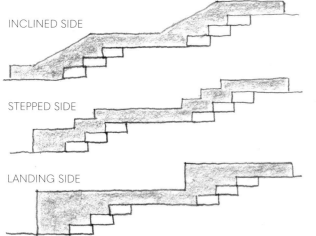

INCLINED SIDE

STEPPED SIDE

LANDING SIDE

45cm
10cm

30cm
15cm

BALUSTRADE DESIGN

When planning your steps you may need to incorporate a solid retaining wall or a handrail for support. How these work with the step layout is important and can alter the look of the steps.

STEP DIMENSIONS

When building steps it is important to consider the rise and tread. The diagram displays two standard dimensions fit for garden use.

TIMBER-EDGED STEPS

WHY

An alternative edging method can be created with steel pegs rammed into the ground, supporting horizontally-placed timber and backfilled with loose material.

Here we demonstrate how a few quality materials can transform this basic construction method into something beautiful.

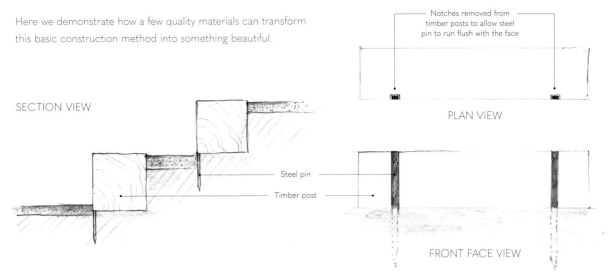

Notches removed from timber posts to allow steel pin to run flush with the face

PLAN VIEW

SECTION VIEW

Steel pin

Timber post

FRONT FACE VIEW

HOW

1: Excavate the ground, clearly defining the outline of the steps.

2: Attach the steel pin to the timber posts and drive them into the ground. Be careful not to damage the appearance of the post.

Use a thin piece of timber between the post and mallet hammer to absorb the impact.

Make sure the posts are lying level.

3: Backfill with soil or a granular sub-base and compact.

4: Place a membrane and a layer of self-binding gravel on top. Aim to keep the level of gravel slightly below the timber to help reduce gravel movement.

Alternatively you can turf in between the posts for a more rustic look.

COBBLES, SLABBING, GRAVEL

The floorscape forms part of the fabric of the garden. The materials, dimensions and their arrangement combine to shape the character and atmosphere of spaces. When deciding on your material choice, there are varying degrees of formality and informality to choose from.

Herringbone bricks provide a more formal decorative look whereas the looseness of an undefined cobbled path with grass encroaching on it provides a more understated effect.

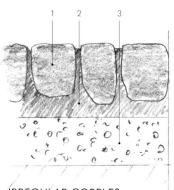

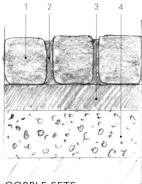

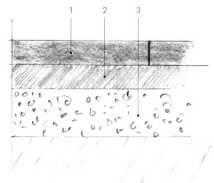

IRREGULAR COBBLES

1: Irregular-sized cobbles

2: Mortar course deeper than the largest cobble depth

3: Granular sub-base

COBBLE SETS

1: Regular-sized cobbles

2: Sharp sand to hold cobbles firm

3: Levelled mortar course

4: Granular sub-base

PAVING SLABS

1: Paving slab

2: Mortar course

3: Granular sub-base

EDGING TECHNIQUES

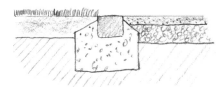

LARGE PAVING STONE

Using a large paving slab creates a strongly defined boundary highlighting the edge as a detail.

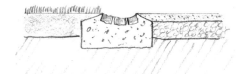

PRONOUNCED TROUGH

A concave cobbled trough adds a traditional character to edging and can be used to catch and direct water runoff.

SUNKEN CURB STONE

Sinking the curb below the finished level of slabs completely hides the curb stone, creating a clean and seamless finish.

STEEL STRIP/GROUND ANCHOR

Using steel edging is a great way of creating an elegant finish, especially when creating curves. These can be anchored into a foundation for strength.

DRY-STONE WALL CONSTRUCTION

HOW

1: Mark out the desired area of your stone wall using a string line and remove turf.

2: Create a stable foundation below ground level using an aggregate sub-base.

3: Lay footing stones on top of the foundation and continue courses until you complete the first lift. Use hearting and pinning stones to fill interior gaps. Choose and maintain a consistent batter angle:

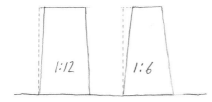

4: Use through stones to span the entire cross-section of the wall, setting these roughly every metre along and halfway up. These keep the wall from splitting and are fundamental to creating a solid structure.

5: Begin the construction of the second lift. Ensure the courses of faced stone are running level. Stones here are typically smaller than those in the first lift. Keep battered angle constant.

6: Once you have reached your desired height finish off the wall by using coping stones. These add additional height and weight to the wall.

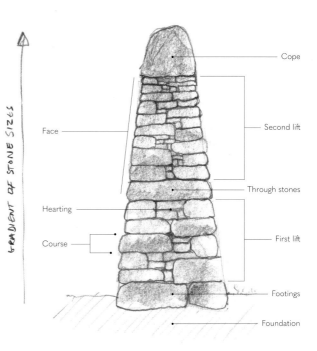

Ensure vertical joints are staggered on the face of the wall to increase rigidity and strength.

COPING METHODS

COCK + HEN COPING STONES

CROPPED COPING STONES

STONE SLAB COPING

UNDERSTANDING STONE

IGNEOUS ROCK

Igneous rocks are formed from the cooling and solidifying of molten magma. They fall into three types:

PLUTONIC ROCKS are created when the magma cools within the earths crust. Important stone groups are **granite**, **syenite**, **diorite** and **gabbro**.

VOLCANIC ROCKS are created when volcanic pressure forces molten magma to the earth's surface where it cools. Best known types are **basalt**, **diabas/dolorite**, **lava tufa**, **pumice stone**, **rhyolite** and **scoria**.

MICROPLUTONIC ROCKS are formed within the earth's crust when low-viscosity magma penetrates cracks in rockfaces. The most important groups are the **pegmatites**, **aplites** and **lamprophyres**.

GENERAL PROPERTIES
Large crystals, visible to the naked eye
Materials that are mixed 'higgledy-piggledy'
Non-directional and compact appearance
No cavities

QUALITIES
High strength
Polish particularly well
Resistant to frost

Resistant to pressure
Resistant to wear
Very dense

SEDIMENTARY ROCK

Sedimentary rocks are formed from sediments that settled at the bottom of a lake, sea or ocean and have been compressed over millions of years.

SANDSTONE is formed when weathered rocks are compacted and particles are cemented in by **clay**, **calcium carbonate** or **silica**.

LIMESTONE + CARBONATES are formed as a result of chemical conditions. Materials such as **lime**, **dolomite** and **gypsum** dissolve in water, break down and form deposits.

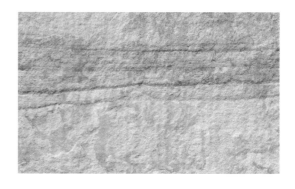

GENERAL PROPERTIES
Layers of sand and minerals
Directional appearance
Very porous

QUALITIES
Weak/moderate strength
Variable rock density
Variable frost resistance
More easily eroded

METAMORPHIC ROCK

Igneous and sedimentary rocks can be shifted into deeper strata by movements in the earth's crust and changed by pressure and high temperatures into a different rock type. This process is called metamorphosis. Important rock types are **quartzite**, **gneiss**, **marble** and **slate**.

QUARTZITES form from the recrystallisation of silica found in sandstone. They are very hard metamorphic rocks with a quartz content of 85%. Their structure makes them easy to split.

MARBLE is a less hard rock as it is composed of calcite. Most marble is made into crushed stone or, as it forms extensive deposits beneath the ground, it can be cut in dimensions suitable for sculptures, buildings and paving.

SLATE is a fine-grained rock created by the alteration of shale or mudstone. It is composed mainly of clay minerals or micas.

GENERAL PROPERTIES
Almost entirely cavity-free
Strongly textured
Foliated texture
Often has a silky sheen

QUALITIES
Polishes to a high lustre
High strength
Variable frost resistance
Pressure resistant
Extremely dense

AVAILABLE STONE FINISHES

	SURFACE FINISHES										
MAGMATITES	Quarry rough	Rough cut	Pointed	Bush hammered	Carved	Chiselled	Sand blasted	Diamond sawn	Polished	Buffed	Flamed
Granite	×	×	×	×				×	×	×	×
Basalt	×	×	×	×				×	×	×	
Diorite	×	×	×	×				×	×	×	
Lava tufa	×	×	×	×	×	×	×	×	×		
SEDIMENTARY											
Quartz sandstone	×	×	×	×	×	×	×	×	×	×	
Sandstone	×	×	×	×	×	×	×	×	×	×	
Dolomite	×	×	×	×	×	×	×	×	×	×	
Limestone	×	×	×	×	×	×	×	×	×	×	
Limestone tufa	×	×	×					×			
METAMORPHITES											
Quartzite	×							×	×	×	
Chlorite slate	×							×	×	×	
Marble	×	×	×	×	×	×	×	×	×	×	
Granulite	×	×	×	×				×	×	×	

FRESHWATER

"We have always been drawn to water. Ystradfellte falls is a beautiful spot. Its lush wooded valleys and riverside trails reveal a succession of waterfalls. We would spend long days here in the summer with Darcy the dog rambling around finding new spots to swim, with a thermos and a few ham sandwiches to hand."

Water is a key element within the landscape. Its reflective qualities are a way of connecting the sky with the earth, adding depth and mystery to a design. It always amazes us how much wildlife is drawn to these habitats, travelling vast distances to find a new breeding ground or just a resting place before the next leg of the journey.

Plants naturalise the boundary with the water and play an essential role in creating a rich and diverse ecosystem. Freshwater habitats are varied: they can be intense and powerful or quiet and tranquil, forge unbeaten routes through the landscape or become the still centre of the garden.

FRESHWATER HABITATS

RIVERS + STREAMS all start at a high point of land and continuously flow in one direction. They all connect together forming a system that flows into either inland bodies of water or the ocean.

LAKES + PONDS represent a freshwater biome type known as a lentic ecosystem, meaning standing or still water. From tiny ponds to huge lakes these freshwater features provide many opportunities for life. A number of distinct natural processes can form lakes:

Tectonic lakes	Ice dam lakes	Oxbow lakes	Glacial lakes
Landslide lakes	Salt lakes	Crater lakes	

BOGS are wetland areas of soft, spongy ground primarily made up of decaying plant matter (peat). The decaying process is lengthened by the waterlogged conditions, as still water holds little oxygen compared to moving water. There are a few distinct types of bog habitat:

Blanket bog	Quaking bog	String bog
Cataract bog	Raised bog	Valley bog

MARSHES develop on low-lying land where water is very close to or above the ground surface for most or part of the year. They can be completely self-contained or occur along the edge of rivers and lakes. These habitats stay soggy even when there are no pools of standing water. There are several types of freshwater marsh:

Wet meadows	Vernal pools	Playa lakes

SWAMPS are forested wetlands where the water fully or partially submerges the vegetation growing around lakes and streams. Water flows very slowly and seasonal rainfall causes the level to fluctuate. Within the swamp, raised areas of ground tend to be drier and support different species of vegetation.

WATER BODY ZONES

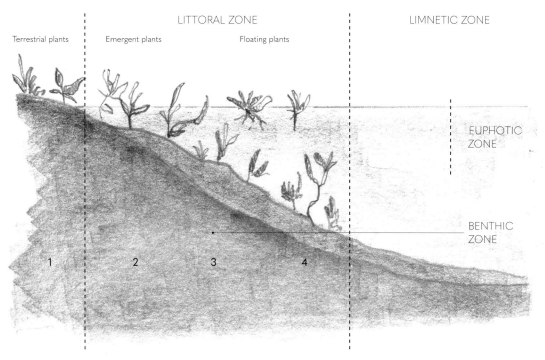

LITTORAL ZONE · LIMNETIC ZONE

Terrestrial plants · Emergent plants · Floating plants

EUPHOTIC ZONE

BENTHIC ZONE

1 · 2 · 3 · 4

1: TERRESTRIAL PLANTS grow on or in the land.

2: EMERGENT PLANTS are rooted within the water but their stems and leaves extend above the surface.

3: FLOATING PLANTS are afloat on the surface. Their roots hang down to filter nutrients from the water that flows by.

4: SUBMERGED PLANTS grow completely under-water.

LITTORAL ZONE

The littoral zone is the area close to the water's edge. The shallow water there lets sunlight penetrate all the way to the sediment, allowing aquatic plants to grow. This can form a narrow or wide fringing wetland with vegetation at various water depths. Many of the animals living within the lakes and rivers depend on the littoral zones of wetlands due to the rich diversity of plant life found there. It is also a good indicator of a healthy habitat.

LIMNETIC ZONE

The limnetic zone is the relatively well lit, open surface water away from the shore. This is too deep to support rooted aquatic plants but is occupied by a variety of photoplankton such as algae, cyanobacteria, zooplankton, small crustaceans and fish. This is the most important zone as it is where photoplankton produce half of the world"s oxygen through the process of photosynthesis.

EUPHOTIC ZONE

The euphotic zone is the layer of water closest to the surface that receives enough light for photosynthesis to occur there.

BENTHIC ZONE

The benthic zone is located at the bottom of a water body. This includes the sediment surface and some sub-surface layers. The organisms that live in this zone are called benthos and are an integral part of the waterland ecosystem.

ELEMENT

DIRECTION

Rivers and streams are defined by direction. Their sole purpose is to flow, relentlessly wearing away the stone below and defining the surrounding landscape.

When introducing moving water into a garden it's often the sound that people first think of, but to us its qualities are more subtle and persuasive. Moving water has the ability to influence your progress around a garden, following its course to a different space which in turn can provide a different atmosphere.

Water flowing relentlessly over Ystradfellte Falls. The majestic sight and sound command attention

Water finds the easiest route downhill, creating a beautiful continuous line. Although it weaves around on the valley floor it projects a very strong sense of direction

The other way of looking at direction is to consider water as a surface that cannot be crossed. This plays a pivotal role in its location within a design. If there is a route across then it possesses a more responsive role, making it an intrinsic part of the garden. If not, then it has the ability to influence the direction you take around a garden space.

It's this connection to plants and wildlife, and interaction with humans, that makes water such an important element within the garden.

ELEMENT
SHAPE

Water habitats are varied, each possessing a different shape and character. When we look at using water within a design its shape is as important as any other quality.

Soft curves give a naturalistic impression. Interplanted with native boggy and marginal plants they have an undefined character, blending in with the extended garden. Straighter, more architectural lines control the shape of water in a more definite way, often turning it into a key element within the design.

Islands are created by the rising water level. The dalmatian pattern of the vegetation fades off into the water, creating a beautifully soft shift from land to water

Water's constant movement shapes the land that surrounds it, creating platforms, pools and islands. It's this relationship with the land, how over time it has become part of the fabric of the river, that is inspiring to us.

Whenever we go to down to the River Wye it's always a rocky outcrop or small beach area that we look for.

The soft curves of this wetland are formed due to the varying depths of the water. The plants hug the shallows, following the contours of the ground. These free-form shapes create open and closed areas

Years of erosion have caused this bedrock to fracture into very harsh and angular pieces. This shape contrasts with the softer, more natural form of the riverbank.

INSPIRATION

MEANDERING
BOARDWALK

EXTENDED
DECK

SOCIAL
SEATING
SPACE

MARGINAL
PLANTING

When walking the perimeter of the lake, appreciating the hazy evening mist, this small inlet of water attracted our eye. For us it offered a resting place, a quiet spot hidden away from the main body of water. It is also a place where plants and wildlife co-exist in the saftey of an enclosed community.

We imagined being able to use this area without damaging it or affecting the native wildlife. Using natural materials was key and raising these above the water allowed life to continue as before beneath. An extended area of deck, enclosed by a low bench, creates a place to rest, and a nearby fork in the road provides an element of choice when continuing along the lakeside route.

When you think of fresh water you think of blue. However, individual colours drawn from from the icy waters of Stickle Tarn evoke a deep and moody atmosphere. This same scene on a sunny summer's day or a fresh spring morning would tell a very different story. Habitats should be appreciated seasonally.

DESIGN CONCEPTS

INSPIRED BY A RIVER'S COURSE

A serpentine rill recedes into the distance, drawing the eye on and through the garden.

Positioning a path to either side helps to emphasise the sinuous shape.

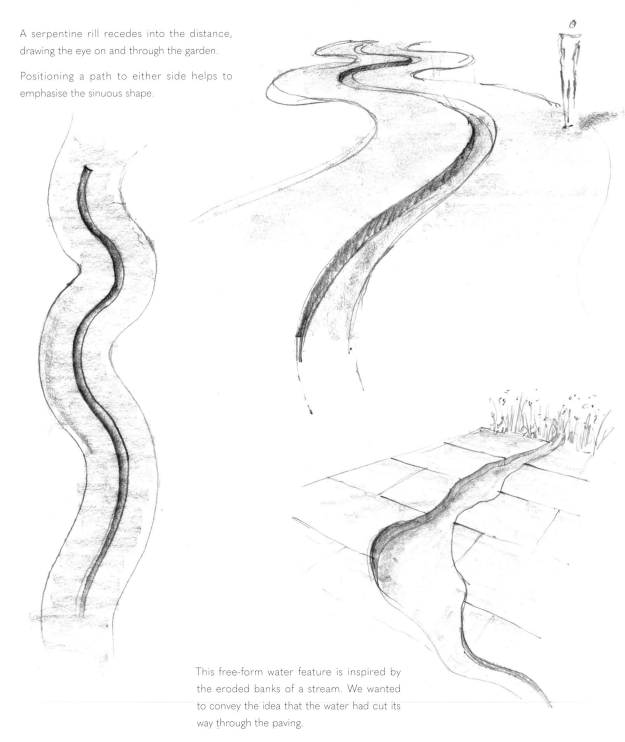

This free-form water feature is inspired by the eroded banks of a stream. We wanted to convey the idea that the water had cut its way through the paving.

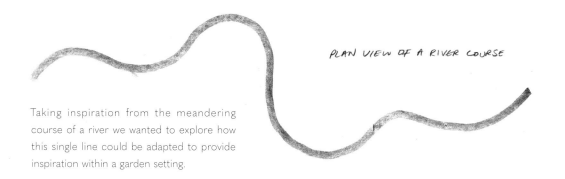

PLAN VIEW OF A RIVER COURSE

Taking inspiration from the meandering course of a river we wanted to explore how this single line could be adapted to provide inspiration within a garden setting.

Here it is as simple as using low hedging to replicate the line. Leaving gaps within the hedge provides points to pass through.

This could be set within a planting bed or out on an open lawn as a minimalistic feature.

The river's shape lends itself to becoming a path. Soft meandering curves lead you through pockets of tall planting to another part of the garden.

Here we use the river's shape as the dividing line between paving and planting, to provide a softer boundary.

INSPIRED BY WATER INTERACTION

Water features don't need to be stand-alone features. Gardens can acquire more depth and meaning by simply connecting a water feature with the surrounding elements, such as paths or planting beds. Here, this concept has been adopted in two contrasting designs.

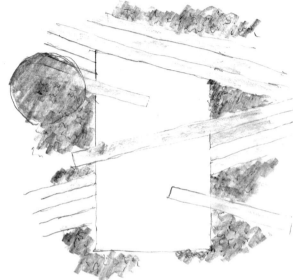

NATURAL

Boulders have been positioned throughout this water feature. Their free form and mass provide a bold display that adds an element of informality. The boulders in the water and on the edge of it connect the two spaces.

The arrangement of rock and water encourages you to go over and sit beside it. This interaction adds depth and meaning to the use of water within the garden.

MODERN

The water feature becomes an integral part of this space with linear walkways passing over it, creating a network of routes. A strong sense of connectedness is created.

Planting beds have been positioned between the walkways, again adding to the overall sense of unity.

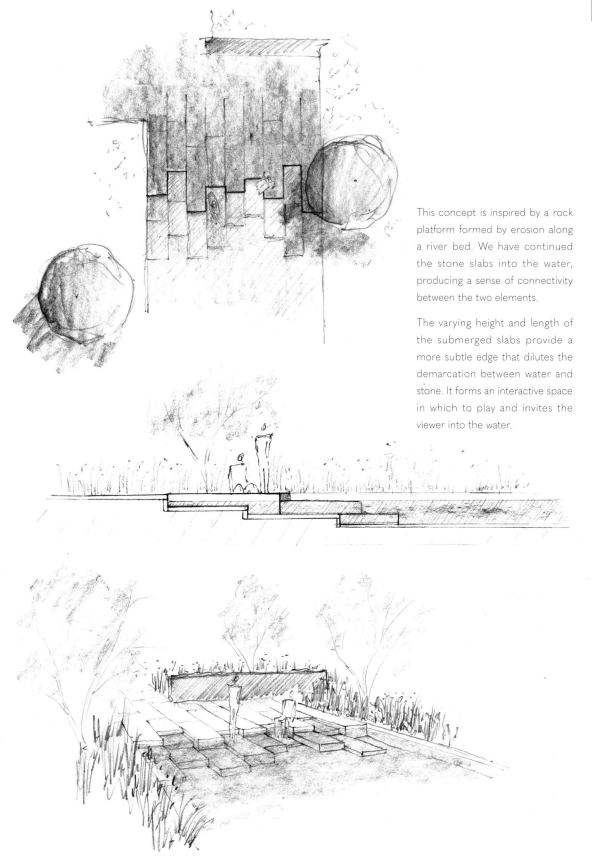

This concept is inspired by a rock platform formed by erosion along a river bed. We have continued the stone slabs into the water, producing a sense of connectivity between the two elements.

The varying height and length of the submerged slabs provide a more subtle edge that dilutes the demarcation between water and stone. It forms an interactive space in which to play and invites the viewer into the water.

INSPIRED BY WATER CROSSINGS

These plans have been inspired by naturally occurring water crossings found within freshwater habitats.

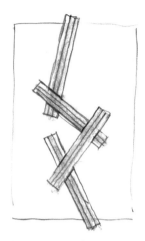

CRACKED ICE

A distinctive composition of angular platforms. This pattern, inspired by cracked ice on a lake, has a modern character. The platforms have been positioned to allow alternative routes over the water.

BOULDERS

Inspired by the positioning of boulders when washed down a river, this use of large stepping stones creates a more natural and sympathetic route across the water.

FALLEN TREES

A fallen tree has always made an exciting route across a stream. Interconnecting wooden planks create a zig-zag journey across the surface of the water.

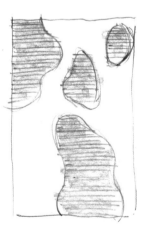

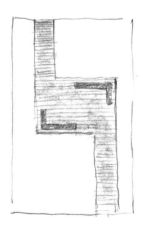

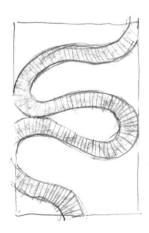

HIGHER GROUND

Areas of higher ground have inspired this route. Their free-form shape creates an undefined route. The islands can be used to cross the water in different directions.

ISLAND

Inspired by an island, we have created a centre platform that provides a quiet spot to sit in whilst surrounded by water.

INVERTED RIVER CROSSING

In contrast to naturally occuring river crossings, we have also been inspired by the river course itself. This path has been designed to be accessible from all four sides, creating an inviting, interactive space.

POSITIONING A WATER FEATURE

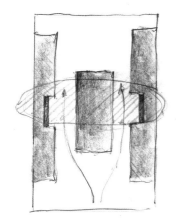

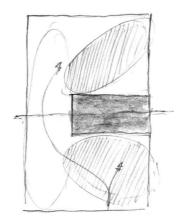

A central water feature creates a prominent element within the garden, leaving perfect places to sit on either side.

This water feature forms a strong division between the two spaces. It dictates a distinctive route down the left-hand side whilst creating two individual spaces in front and behind.

Locating the water feature on the far wall allows the rest of the garden to be left open. By distancing the water feature you have less of an immediate association with it.

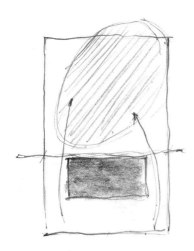

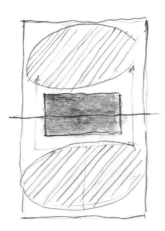

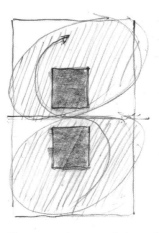

By locating the water feature at the front of the garden it becomes more prominent. You are forced to engage with it to travel to the larger space at the far end of the garden.

Here, the water feature's position and orientation create a balanced yet bold concept. The routes to either side of the water feature are narrower, emphasising the division between the front and rear spaces. This creates a disruption between the two but retains a visual connection.

The same size overall, here the water feature has been split in half to create a more interactive space, encouraging you to walk between the two bodies of water.

INSPIRED BY BOULDERS

A water feature doesn't have to be left bare. By simply positioning objects within, it becomes more textured.

These natural boulders sit firmly within the water, anchoring them to the space and bringing a sense of age to the scene.

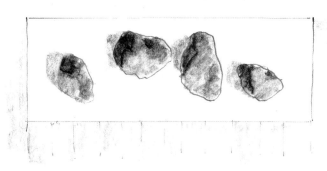

Here, continuing cobbles down into a water feature creates a more seamless appearance.

This detail allows the water feature to fuse with the surrounding design whilst creating the impression of a body of water that has risen from the ground.

"... Life gets busier but there is always time to get together and do the simple things ... Andy, Eddy and Fuz went to school with us,
shared an adventure around the world, and take every opportunity to catch up when our hectic lives allow it ..."

A FRESHWATER GARDEN

INITIAL CONCEPT

RIVER ZONE

Potential for water to continue through the divide

Very private, intimate space; very natural

Denser tree canopy

A change in level to enable a river course through the landscape

A strong division to completely isolate the rear of the garden

LAKE ZONE

Central area to be occupied by water imitating a lake

A large dominant feature, softened either side with planting, trees and shrubs

Potential for unique walkway across

MARSH ZONE

A more open area for seating, organic-shaped planting beds echoing the appearance of a marsh

Very soft and natural

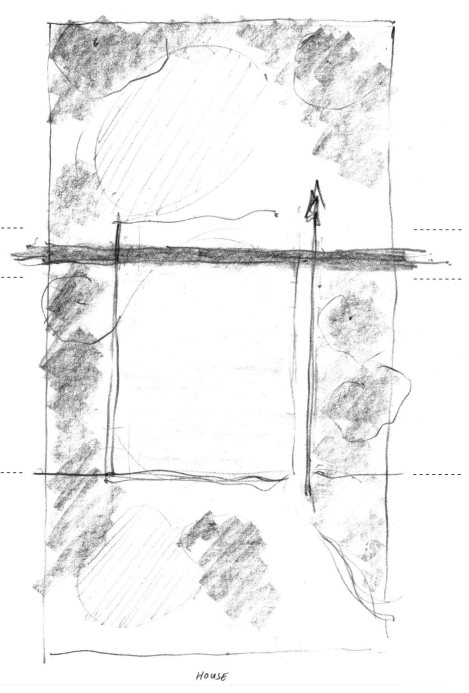

HOUSE

CONCEPT DEVELOPMENT

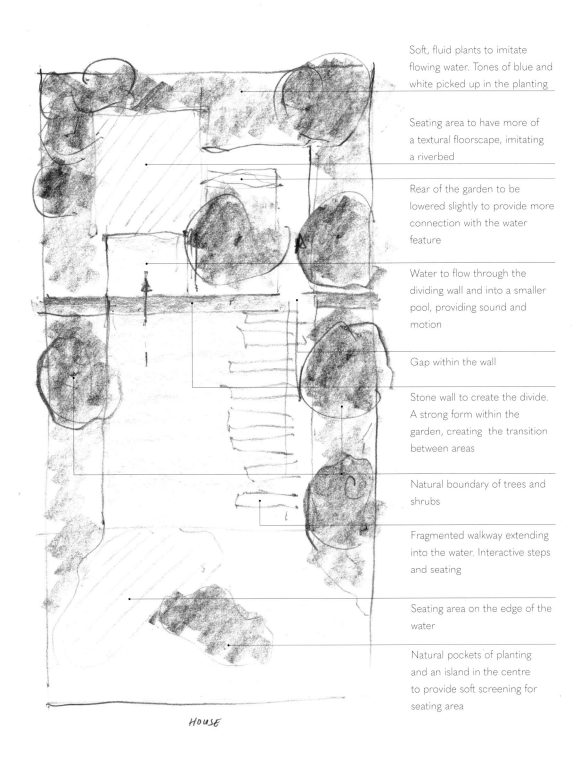

Soft, fluid plants to imitate flowing water. Tones of blue and white picked up in the planting

Seating area to have more of a textural floorscape, imitating a riverbed

Rear of the garden to be lowered slightly to provide more connection with the water feature

Water to flow through the dividing wall and into a smaller pool, providing sound and motion

Gap within the wall

Stone wall to create the divide. A strong form within the garden, creating the transition between areas

Natural boundary of trees and shrubs

Fragmented walkway extending into the water. Interactive steps and seating

Seating area on the edge of the water

Natural pockets of planting and an island in the centre to provide soft screening for seating area

HOUSE

CONCEPT DEVELOPMENT

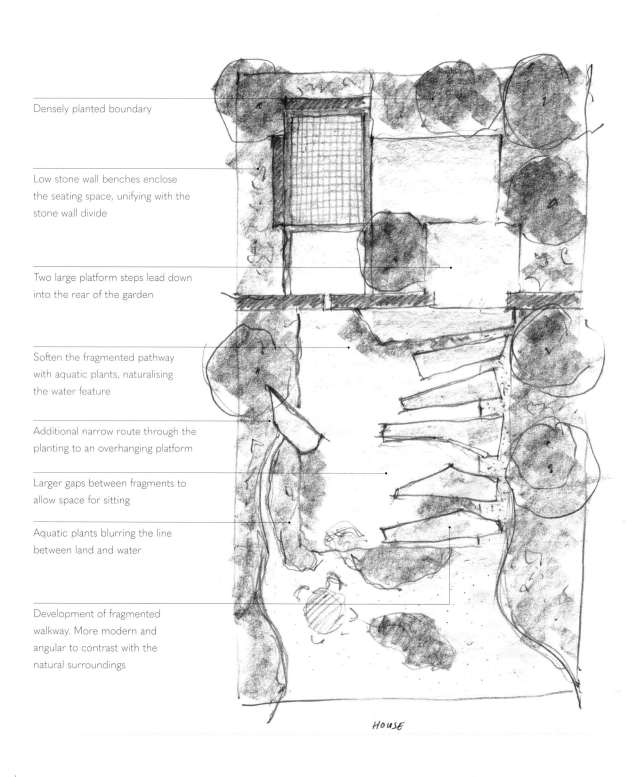

Densely planted boundary

Low stone wall benches enclose the seating space, unifying with the stone wall divide

Two large platform steps lead down into the rear of the garden

Soften the fragmented pathway with aquatic plants, naturalising the water feature

Additional narrow route through the planting to an overhanging platform

Larger gaps between fragments to allow space for sitting

Aquatic plants blurring the line between land and water

Development of fragmented walkway. More modern and angular to contrast with the natural surroundings

HOUSE

FINAL DESIGN

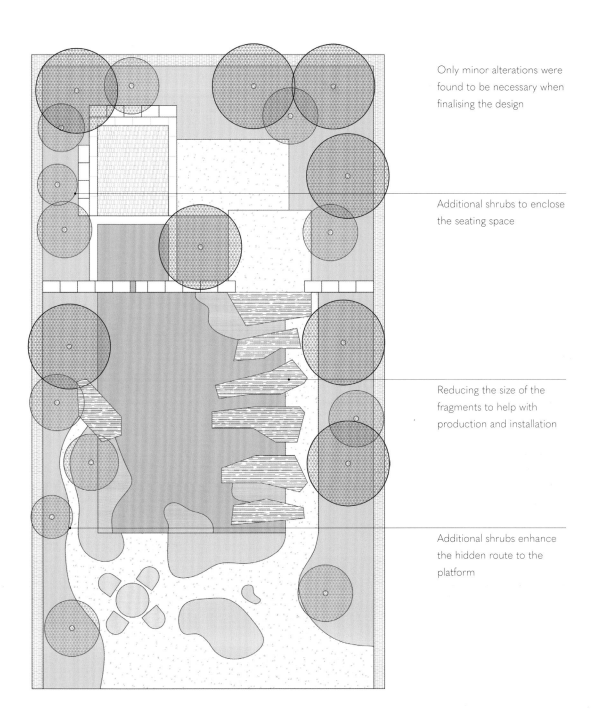

Only minor alterations were found to be necessary when finalising the design

Additional shrubs to enclose the seating space

Reducing the size of the fragments to help with production and installation

Additional shrubs enhance the hidden route to the platform

FINAL DESIGN VISUALS

The section view below clearly shows the three distinct areas within the garden. Directly outside the house the ground is open, allowing views to extend all the way to the rear. The fragmented platforms extend out into the water providing a choice of routes, one being very easy and functional and the other requiring more thought and interaction.

At the rear of the garden the subtle drop in level allows the water to pass through the wall and fall into a separate pool. A change in floorscape creates a more textured and natural character to the space.

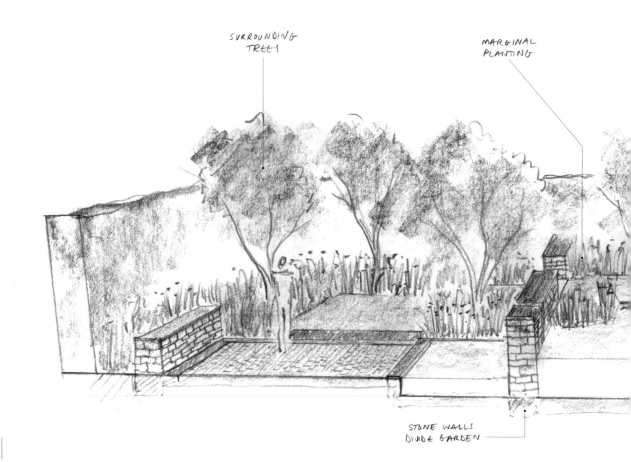

SURROUNDING TREES

MARGINAL PLANTING

STONE WALLS DIVIDE GARDEN

WATER FEATURE

STONE WALL

STONE BENCH

COBBLED FLOOR DETAIL

Looking from the rear of the garden back towards the house reveals a very different character to the design.

The detail of the stone becomes a dominant feature of the garden, complementing the soft natural planting surrounding it.

FRAGMENTED PLATFORMS

FRESHWATER PLANTING

Planting is fundamental when creating a well-balanced and natural water habitat that attracts a diverse range of indigenous wildlife.

Whenever we visit lakes and rivers around Wales we take time to explore the marginal planting that softens the division between land and water. Plants can form large drifts that hug the shallows, meander down a river's course or reveal isolated islands in boggy terrain.

Boggy margins support a wide range of plants just above the waterline, their texture, form and size add depth and structure to a scheme. Grasses bring vertical accents to the display and their flowerheads bend in the wind, bringing movement to the scene.

A boggy or marginal planting bed provides the opportunity to use some beautiful native and ornamental plants such as Eupatorium with its dense domed clusters of tiny light pink flowers or Rodgersia, whose jagged palmate leaves bring an architectural quality to the edge of the water.

IMITATING A FRESHWATER PLANTING SCHEME

CONCEPT DESIGN

We wanted to create a large pond that was planted up with native and ornamental plants, such as Darmera peltata, which displays vase-like leaves, and the contrasting dense spires of deep yellow flowers on black stems of Ligularia przewalskii. The Royal fern Osmunda regalis nestles amongst these bog-loving plants, its bright green fronds accentuated by the yellow flowers of Iris psuedacorus.

Our marginal planting consists predominantly of native grasses, lending a natural character to the scheme. Carex pendula with its tall arching stems and earthy yellow pendant flowerheads knits the marginal area together, contrasting with stalks of light purple flowers from Stachys palustris.

Water hawthorn Aponogeton distachyos has been chosen as a deep marginal. Its small, white, vanilla-scented flowers are revealed in late winter and spring, picking up where it left off in the autumn and flowering until the pond freezes. A dwarf waterlily provides the perfect planting companion, displaying isolated white flowers in the summer months.

DP	**Elephant's ears** Darmera peltata		SP	**Marsh woundwort** Stachys palustris
OR	**Royal fern** Osmunda regalis		AD	**Water hawthorn** Aponogeton distachyos
LP	**Ligularia** Ligularia przewalskii			**Weeping sedge** Carex pendula
IP	**Yellow flag iris** Iris pseudacorus			**Dwarf white waterlily** Nymphaea candida

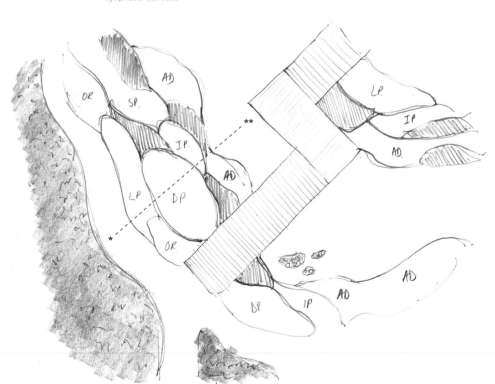

DEVELOPED DESIGN

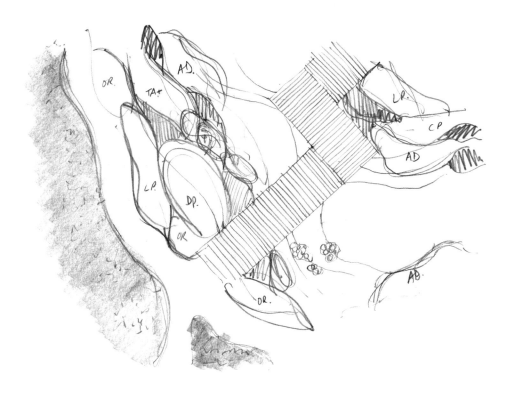

SECTIONAL VIEW THROUGH PLANTING SCHEME

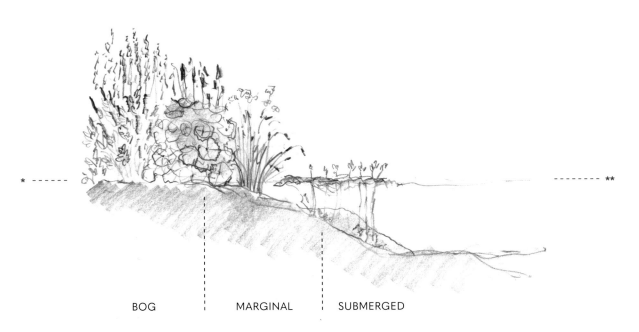

BOG   MARGINAL   SUBMERGED

BOG-LOVING

PLANT SELECTIONS

Elephant's ears / Chilean rhubarb
Darmera peltata

A clump-forming herbaceous perennial with large glossy, rounded leaves that turn from deep green to red in autumn. It is native to the US where it is found growing on the banks of woodland streams. En masse this plant makes a big statement in a boggy area. Flowers arrive in spring before the leaves.

HEIGHT ↕ 1.5m SPREAD ↔ 1m FLOWERING ❀ APR
POSITION ☼ FULL SUN ◐ PARTIAL SHADE HARDINESS ❸ ❹ ❺ **❻** ❼

Royal fern
Osmunda regalis

Tough, large deciduous fern forming a clump of architectural fronds. It provides a fresh burst of green in spring and then browns off in autumn. A rusty-brown spore emerges between the fronds, giving a rustic, earthy character. Grows best in acid soil and can tolerate sun and shade and an exposed site.

HEIGHT ↕ 2m SPREAD ↔ 4m FLOWERING ❀ JUN
POSITION ◐ PARTIAL SHADE HARDINESS ❸ ❹ ❺ **❻** ❼

Rodgersia
Rodgersia podophylla

From the damp shady woodlands of Japan, this robust herbaceous perennial forms a clump of jagged palmate leaves, which start off a rich brown and turn green. Grows best in a poorly drained clay or loam soil and in a sheltered spot.

HEIGHT ↕ 1.5m SPREAD ↔ 1.8m FLOWERING ❀ JUL-AUG
POSITION ☼ FULL SUN ◐ PARTIAL SHADE HARDINESS ❸ ❹ ❺ **❻** ❼

LIgularia 'The Rocket'
Ligularia przewalskii 'The Rocket'

A vigorous clump-forming deciduous perennial with elegant spikes of golden-yellow flowers on dark stems and just as striking leaves. Grows in most soil types provided they are poorly drained. Does best in a sheltered spot.

HEIGHT ↕ 1.8m SPREAD ↔ 1m FLOWERING ❀ JUL-AUG
POSITION ☼ FULL SUN HARDINESS ❸ ❹ ❺ **❻** ❼

❸ hardy in coastal and relatively mild parts of the UK [-5 to 1°C]
❹ hardy through most of the UK [-10 to -5°C]
❺ hardy in most places throughout the UK, even in severe winters [-15 to -10°C]
❻ hardy in all of UK and northern Europe [-20 to -15°C]
❼ hardy in the severest European continental climates [-20°C and lower]

SUBMERGED

PLANT SELECTIONS

Narrow-leaved arrowhead

Sagittaria graminea

A herbaceous submerged or marginal aquatic perennial that requires little maintenance. Spreads along the ground to create an evergreen cover. A really tolerant plant that can grow in natural, clay or silt soils.

HEIGHT ↕ 0.3m SPREAD ↔ 0.6m FLOWERING ✻ JUN-JUL
POSITION ☀ FULL SUN ⛅ PARTIAL SHADE WATER DEPTH 4-10cm
HARDINESS 3 4 5 **6** 7

Dwarf white waterlily

Nymphaea candida

A herbaceous perennial with beautiful white cupped flowers. It has a compact growth habit so is perfect for smaller ponds. Very elegant and understated leaves and flowers make this a really special plant.

HEIGHT ↕ 0.1m SPREAD ↔ 0.6m FLOWERING ✻ JUL-AUG
POSITION ☀ FULL SUN WATER DEPTH 15-25cm
HARDINESS 3 **4** 5 6 7

Water hawthorn

Aponogeton distachyos

This exotic-looking deciduous aquatic originates from South Africa. It's dormant in summer so is great for planting alongside waterlilies. Emerges from the water to produce elliptical leaves and delicate white flowers which can appear twice in the year. Grows in most soils and tolerates an exposed pond.

HEIGHT ↕ 0.1m SPREAD ↔ 1m FLOWERING ✻ MAR-JUL, SEP-DEC
POSITION ☀ FULL SUN ⛅ PARTIAL SHADE WATER DEPTH 30-90cm
HARDINESS 3 4 5 **6** 7

Water violet

Hottonia palustris

An aquatic perennial that helps to keep your pond water well oxygenated. Foliage grows completely submerged but the long flower spikes emerge bearing a set of light purple flowers. Requires strong light and cooler waters. Works well in large or small ponds.

HEIGHT ↕ 0.5m SPREAD ↔ 1m FLOWERING ✻ MAY/AUG
POSITION ☀ FULL SUN WATER DEPTH 10-20cm
HARDINESS 3 4 **5** 6 7

MARGINAL

PERENNIALS

Yellow flag iris

Iris pseudacorus

A vigorous deciduous perennial that can spread to form extensive colonies, so is only recommended in large ponds. Stunning yellow flowers amongst upright grey-green leaves. Grows in clay and loam provided they're poorly drained. Can tolerate an exposed area.

HEIGHT ↕ 1m SPREAD ↔ 1.5m FLOWERING ❀ JUL-AUG
POSITION ☼ FULL SUN ☼ PARTIAL SHADE WATER DEPTH 5-25cm
HARDINESS [3] [4] [5] [6] **[7]**

Swamp lily

Saururus cernuus

Has a beautiful clump of dark green, heart-shaped leaves. A deciduous perennial with a natural character. Fragrant spikes of nodding white flowers emerge in summer. This plant is invasive so does require maintenance. Grows in most soil types and sheltered or exposed sites.

HEIGHT ↕ 1.5m SPREAD ↔ 0.5m FLOWERING ❀ JUN-AUG
POSITION ☼ FULL SUN ☼ PARTIAL SHADE WATER DEPTH 0-6cm
HARDINESS [3] [4] [5] [6] **[7]**

Water forget-me-not

Myosotis scorpioides

Unlike garden forget-me-nots this is a reliable perennial that spreads gradually, while not invasive. Forms large clumps that can be divided every few years. Can be planted on the edge of the water or in a reliably moist bog garden. Grows in most soils as long as they are poorly drained.

HEIGHT ↕ 0.5m SPREAD ↔ 0.5m FLOWERING ❀ JUN-AUG
POSITION ☼ FULL SUN ☼ PARTIAL SHADE WATER DEPTH 0-20cm
HARDINESS [3] [4] [5] **[6]** [7]

Wild angelica

Angelica sylvestris

This short-lived perennial provides an architectural display. Umbels of tiny white flowers sit above tall upright stems. The flowers provide a frothy appearance that will self-seed. Prefers a heavier, poorly-drained soil.

HEIGHT ↕ 2m SPREAD ↔ 1m FLOWERING ❀ JUL-SEP
POSITION ☼ FULL SUN ☼ PARTIAL SHADE WATER DEPTH 0-2cm
HARDINESS [3] [4] **[5]** [6] [7]

Weeping sedge
Carex pendula

A native sedge that forms dense clumps of tough, dark evergreen foliage. It's perfect to grow in more tricky spots but will self-seed. This tufted grass grows in damp clay or loam soils.

HEIGHT ↕ 1.2m SPREAD ↔ 1m FLOWERING ❀ MAY-OCT
POSITION ☀ FULL SUN ⛅ PARTIAL SHADE WATER DEPTH 0-4cm
HARDINESS 3 4 5 **6** 7

Lesser bulrush
Typha angustifolia

This tall deciduous native grass is only recommended for large ponds as it can be invasive. Elegant and architectural with cylindrical brown flower spikes that are pollinated by wind. Attracts plenty of wildlife and grows in any soil type and exposed sites.

HEIGHT ↕ 1.5m SPREAD ↔ 1.5m FLOWERING ❀ APR-MAY
POSITION ☀ FULL SUN ⛅ PARTIAL SHADE WATER DEPTH 10-50cm
HARDINESS 3 4 **5** 6 7

Common cotton grass
Eriophorum angustifolium

A spreading perennial that forms tufts of dark green leaves. Found in open wetlands, heath or moorland, it prefers an acid soil but will grow in most other types. Begins to flower in May displaying a distinctive white bristle-like flower that resembles tufts of cotton.

HEIGHT ↕ 0.5m SPREAD ↔ 1.5m FLOWERING ❀ APR-JUN
POSITION ☀ FULL SUN WATER DEPTH 0-6cm
HARDINESS 3 4 5 6 **7**

Reed canary grass
Phalaris arundinacea

This grass commonly forms extensive single-species strands along the margins of lakes and streams in wet open areas. The blade-like leaves are usually green but can variegate. Can tolerate slightly drier sites.

HEIGHT ↕ 1.5m SPREAD ↔ 4m FLOWERING ❀ JUN/OCT
POSITION ☀ FULL SUN WATER DEPTH 0-60cm
HARDINESS 3 4 5 6 **7**

OXYGENATING

PLANT SELECTIONS

Water crowfoot

Ranunculus aquatilis

This pretty perennial forms a mat of evergreen foliage on the water's surface. Foliage grows best in gently moving waters. White-petalled flowers grow a centimetre or two above the toothed leaves. Grows in most soils and can tolerate an exposed water surface.

HEIGHT ↕ 0.1m SPREAD ↔ 0.5m FLOWERING ❋ APR–MAY
POSITION ☼ FULL SUN ◐ PARTIAL SHADE WATER DEPTH 10–60cm
HARDINESS 3 4 5 6 **7**

Spiked water milfoil

Myriophyllum spicatum

Only growing in still or slow-moving waters, this herbaceous aquatic forms dense mats beneath the surface. It has long, slender branching stems of bright green leaves. It can crowd out other plants within your pond so may require maintenance.

HEIGHT ↕ 0.1m SPREAD ↔ 1.5m FLOWERING ❋ JUN–JUL
POSITION ☼ FULL SUN WATER DEPTH 30–200cm
HARDINESS 3 **4** 5 6 7

Curled pondweed

Potamogeton crispus

A submerged native oxygenator with evergreen fern-like olive-green leaves. It is non-invasive and can tolerate a shaded area and provides great homes for amphibians. It is frost hardy and can grow in natural clay or silt soils.

HEIGHT ↕ 0.5m SPREAD ↔ 1m FLOWERING ❋ MAY–OCT
POSITION ☼ FULL SUN ◐ PARTIAL SHADE WATER DEPTH 30–60cm
HARDINESS 3 4 **5** 6 7

Floating four-leaf clover

Marsilea quadrifolia

This is actually an aquatic fern with simple four-lobed leaves. Its colour and growth habit vary in different conditions. The leaves float on the surface even in deep water but if grown in the shallows, they may raise from the water slightly. Prefers a light sandy or medium loamy soil.

HEIGHT ↕ 0.1m SPREAD ↔ 0.3m WATER DEPTH 0–25cm
POSITION ☼ FULL SUN ◐ PARTIAL SHADE HARDINESS 3 4 **5** 6 7

WATER MEADOW

PLANTING MIX

Many low-lying areas within a garden can be damp and hard to manage. This meadow mix includes species that will thrive in moist conditions. You can also use this mix at the edge of ponds, riverbanks and in ditches.

PRIMARY SPECIES

↑ Rough-stalked meadow grass
Poa trivialis

Slender creeping red fescue
Festuca rubra litoralis

Crested dog's tail
Cynosurus cristatus

Tall fescue
Festuca arundinacea

Tufted hair grass
Deschampsia cespitosa

Smaller cat's tail
Phleum bertolonii

SECONDARY SPECIES

↑ Hemp agrimony
Eupatorium cannabinum

Creeping buttercup
Ranunculus repens

Meadow buttercup
Ranunculus acris

Ox-eye daisy
Leucanthemum vulgare

Salad burnet
Sanguisorba minor

Meadowsweet
Filipendula ulmaria

Yellow flag
Iris pseudacorus

Purple loosestrife
Lythrum salicaria

TERTIARY SPECIES

↑ Great burnet
Sanguisorba officinalis

Yellow rattle
Rhinanthus minor

Greater birdsfoot
Lotus uliginosus

Autumn hawkbit
Scorzoneroides autumnalis

Ragged robin
Lychnis flos-cuculi

Gypsywort
Lycopus europaeus

Devil's bit scabious
Succisa pratensis

Marsh marigold
Caltha palustris

Common fleabane
Pulicaria dysenterica

Hard rush
Juncus inflexus

SHRUB

SELECTIONS

Alder buckthorn
Rhamnus frangula

Naturally found in hedgerows this deciduous shrub will develop into a small tree if left. It is a tough species that tolerates all soil types provided they're poorly-drained; can tolerate a windy site. Provides a display of yellow and red-purple berries in autumn.

HEIGHT ↕ 5m+ SPREAD ↔ 5m FLOWERING ❋ APR–MAY
POSITION ☀ FULL SUN ◐ PARTIAL SHADE HARDINESS [3] [4] [5] [6] **[7]**

Button bush
Cephalanthus occidentalis

Actually part of the coffee family, it is a common shrub in many wetland habitats including swamps, floodplains and moist forest understoreys. This bushy deciduous shrub displays green oval leaves on open branching stems, red when young. Displays fragrant tubular flowers carried in a dense ball.

HEIGHT ↕ 2m SPREAD ↔ 2m FLOWERING ❋ JUN
POSITION ☀ FULL SUN ◐ PARTIAL SHADE HARDINESS [3] [4] **[5]** [6] [7]

Guelder rose
Viburnum opulus

An upright deciduous shrub with palmate leaves that turn a vivid pink-red in autumn. Often grown for its flower, it also boasts three-lobed leaves, long and broad with serrated margins, and its fruits are bright red. Grows in all soil types and moist or well-drained soils. Tolerates an exposed position.

HEIGHT ↕ 4m SPREAD ↔ 4m FLOWERING ❋ MAY–JUN
POSITION ☀ FULL SUN ◐ PARTIAL SHADE HARDINESS [3] [4] [5] **[6]** [7]

Possumhaw holly
Ilex decidua

Bunches of small red berries cling tightly to the bare branches in late autumn. These berries remain untill spring unless eaten by birds. Possumhaw naturally suckers from the roots so it's best to allow for multi-stem growth.

HEIGHT ↕ 2m+ SPREAD ↔ 2m+ FLOWERING ❋ MAY
POSITION ☀ FULL SUN ◐ PARTIAL SHADE HARDINESS [3] [4] **[5]** [6] [7]

TREE

SELECTIONS

Goat willow
Salix caprea

Medium-sized tree that unlike most willows develops oval-shaped leaves. Its flowers appear amongst the earliest in the year, providing valuable food for foraging bees. Thrives in wet conditions though can tolerate drier soils.

HEIGHT ↕ 10m SPREAD ↔ 8m FLOWERING ✿ MAR–APR
POSITION ☼ FULL SUN HARDINESS [3] [4] [5] [6] [7]

River birch
Betula nigra

A large deciduous tree best known for its beautiful peeling bark. It bears simple ovate leaves along with attractive yellow catkins that emerge in spring. Its native habitat is wet ground though it will tolerate higher, drier ground and once established is one of the few birches that can tolerate heat well.

HEIGHT ↕ 20m SPREAD ↔ 5m+ FLOWERING ✿ APR–MAY
POSITION ☼ FULL SUN ◐ PARTIAL SHADE HARDINESS [3] [4] [5] [6] [7]

Bird cherry
Prunus padus

Found in the wild within wet woodlands and on streams and riverbanks, this is a beautiful tree to have near the water's edge. This large, bushy deciduous tree displays ovate leaves that turn yellow in autumn and a covering of fragrant white flowers in late spring. Grows in any soil type and can thrive in exposed sites.

HEIGHT ↕ 10m SPREAD ↔ 8m+ FLOWERING ✿ APR
POSITION ☼ FULL SUN ◐ PARTIAL SHADE HARDINESS [3] [4] [5] [6] [7]

Grey alder
Alnus incana

A fast-growing upright deciduous tree that can be found in the wild in boggy riversides or rocky mountainsides. A simple understated tree, a natural beauty. Grows in most soil conditions and exposed sites.

HEIGHT ↕ 20m SPREAD ↔ 8m+ FLOWERING ✿ FEB
POSITION ☼ FULL SUN HARDINESS [3] [4] [5] [6] [7]

CREATING A NATURAL POND

Roughly 2,500 years ago at least a quarter of Britain would have been wetland, but due to population growth, that area has dramatically reduced. Natural ponds support up to two-thirds of all freshwater species, an incredible amount, which makes it a priority to sustain this habitat.

SIZE

A pond can be any size though the bigger it is the better as it can support a wider range of plants and animals, increasing the biodiversity of the habitat.

POSITION

Choose a level, light and sunny spot away from too many overhanging trees. It's best to avoid a wet hollow as it may flood during wet weather. Surrounding vegetation will help to encourage wildlife and enhance a naturalistic feeling.

SURROUNDING POLLUTION

It is important your pond remains clean, providing a healthy environment for the plants and animals living in it. Be mindful of any nearby pollution sources that could affect your pond's ecosystem.

THINGS NOT TO DO

Don't introduce ornamental fish as they will eat tadpoles and other small invertebrates. Avoid planting invasive species as these can take over your pond and even escape into the natural waterways.

INVASIVE NATIVE PLANTS

only recommended for larger ponds:

Floating sweet-grass
Glyceria fluitans

Reedmaces
Typha latifolia
Typha angustifolia

Yellow/White waterlily
Nymphaea alba

Fringed waterlily
Nymphoides peltata

Lesser spearwort
Ranunculus flammula

Greater spearwort
Ranunculus lingua

Bogbean
Menyanthes trifoliata

PROBLEM	ORIGIN	SOLUTION
Duckweed	Chemical or nutrient imbalance.	Remove duckweed or stock with extra plants to oxygenate and shade out the weed.
Blanketweed	Increase in light levels before other plants begin to grow. Not a problem in larger ponds.	Remove blanketweed with a stick. Leave this beside the pond for a few days allowing any pond creatures to find their way back.
Green water	Occurs naturally in new ponds due to excess nutrients in tap water. May occur in spring with increased light levels.	In a new pond, leave for 1–2 weeks. If the problem persists, add barley straw in hessian sacks. The barley breaks down and releases chemicals which inhibit the growth of algae. This works best in summer when the water is warmer.
Brown water	Caused by low levels of oxygen and high levels of nutrients.	Add barley straw in hessian sacks, or you can add pollutant-tolerant oxygenators such as yellow/white waterlily and broad-leaved pondweed.
Punctured liner	Stones, roots, other sharp objects.	Epoxy compounds and patches are available.
Rampant vegetation	Exotic plants that cannot be controlled by native fauna.	Remove by hand.
Frogs disappearing	Being eaten by fish or other wildlife.	Provide more habitats such as logs, stones, boulders, taller plants.
Dead frogs	Frogs can die of exhaustion after spawning. They can catch diseases such as red leg and if they overwinter in the pond they can become frozen.	This is natural!
Grass and leaves blowing into pond		Make sure you have planting on the banks of your pond. This will catch grass and leaves and also any loose rubbish.
Frozen pond		Place a pan of warm water on the surface to melt a hole in the ice. This is not a problem in larger ponds, where wildlife will survive much longer.

PLANTING ZONES – MARGINAL SHELVES

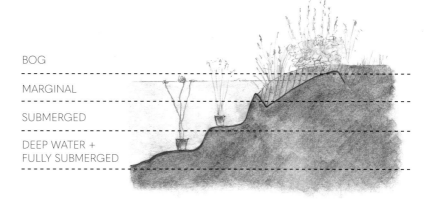

BOG
- -
MARGINAL
- -
SUBMERGED
- -
DEEP WATER +
FULLY SUBMERGED
- -

This diagram displays the separate planting zones within a pond. Having plants in each zone is best for your pond.

MARGINAL   0–15cm

These plants are best suited to being positioned on the water's edge or to a depth of 15cm. They thrive in wet mud, boggy conditions, stream edge or shallow water.

MARGINAL   15–25cm

These marginal plants can be separated into two categories: ones that spread horizontally across the water's surface and emergent plants that grow vertically up and out of the water.

SUBMERGED   25–45cm

At this depth range plants should be provided with a deeper shelf that keeps the crown of the plant in the water throughout winter.

SUBMERGED AND FLOATING   > 45cm

To create a well-balanced pond it's key to have submerged oxygenating plants, waterlilies or floating plants: 50–70% of the pond surface should be covered by plants. This keeps the water shady in the summer and is fundamental to increasing its clarity.

BRITISH NATIVE PLANTS FOR ALL PLANTING ZONES

BOG

Marsh marigold
Caltha palustris

Hemp agrimony
Eupatorium cannabinum

Meadowsweet
Filipendula ulmaria

Water avens
Geum rivale

Yellow flag iris
Iris pseudacorus

Ragged robin
Lychnis flos-cuculi

Loosestrife
Lythrum salicaria

Cowslip
Primula veris

Devil's bit scabious
Succisa pratensis

Brooklime
Veronica beccabunga

0–15cm

Marsh marigold
Caltha palustris

Greater pond sedge
Carex riparia

Cotton grass
Eriophorum angustifolium

Loosestrife
Lythrum salicaria

Water mint
Mentha aquatica

Bog bean
Menyanthes trifoliata

Water forget-me-not
Myosotis scorpioides

Marsh cinquefoil
Potentilla palustris

Watercress
Rorippa nasturtium-aquaticum

Greater spearwort
Ranunculus flammula

15–25cm

Water plantain
Alisma plantago-aquatica

Flowering rush
Butomus umbellatus

Starwort
Callitriche palustris

Sweet galingale
Cyperus longus

Slender club rush
Isolepis cernua

Arrowhead
Sagittaria sagittifolia

Common club rush
Schoenoplectus lacustris

25–45cm

Hornwort
Ceratophyllum demersum

Water moss
Fontinalis antipyretica

Frogbit
Hydrocharis morsus-ranae

Spiked milfoil
Myriophyllum spicatum

Curled pondweed
Potamogeton crispus

Water crowfoot
Ranunculus aquatilis

>45cm

Pond waterlily
Nymphaea alba

Water soldier
Stratiotes aloides

NATURAL POND DESIGN

We have designed a free-form natural pond with softly curved edges. The bottom of the pond wraps around the land, isolating it and give the impression of an island.

Carefully positioned trees, shrubs and marginal planting on the banks of the pond obscure the eyeline down the length of the pond, creating the illusion that the pond is larger than it is.

We have positioned a boardwalk across the width of the pond. It's disjointed to provide a larger area to sit on and enjoy different views of the water.

Three individual deep sections are broken up by shallow shelves bridging the water. As the pond establishes these shallower levels will allow plants to fuse together, creating individual pools.

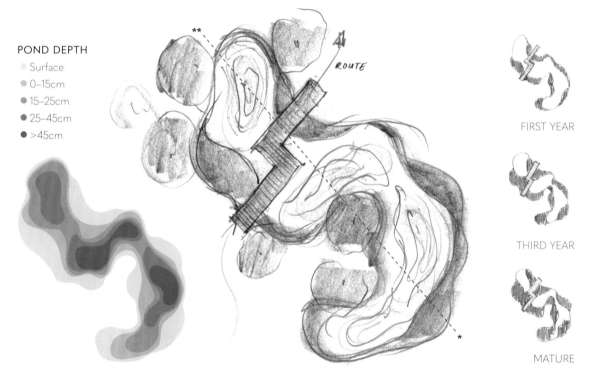

POND DEPTH
- Surface
- 0–15cm
- 15–25cm
- 25–45cm
- >45cm

ROUTE

FIRST YEAR

THIRD YEAR

MATURE

A cross-section through the length of the pond (below) shows the variation of depths, providing many different potential habitats and zones for planting.

The desired progression of plants over time is shown above. Plants are confined to the shallower parts of the pond, leaving the deeper pools clear.

NATURAL POND CONSTRUCTION

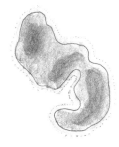

1: Draw out the shape of the pond with line marker and excavate to the required depths.

Plot the positions of the upright posts for the boardwalk. At these points dig out the soil and create a concrete footing. Make the area of the pads larger than you need, approx. 500×500mm and 150–200mm deep.

2: Place an underlay protection course over the top of the concrete footings, smoothing off any sharp edges first.

Lay out an underlay protection layer over the whole area of the pond. Leave excess around the edges and cut to shape.

On top of this, lay out the EPDM liner. Make sure this extends further than the underlay otherwise there is a risk of water being absorbed out of the pond. Overlay another layer of protection.

3: Dig a channel around the pond perimeter. Cut the top protection layer and liner to shape and feed it into the channel. Make sure the two protection layers are completely separate. Place soil back on top to keep it secure.

Build up from the footings with engineering bricks. Two courses is plenty. The upright supports of the boardwalk will be attached to this.

Cover the banks of the pond with soil, approximately 200mm deep. There is no need to cover the bottom as this will build up with sediment naturally.

4: After the brick foundation has set, attach the upright posts to the correct height and begin the construction of the wooden boardwalk.

5: Once the boardwalk is complete, begin to fill up the pond. Place the hosepipe at the lowest level as the rising water will disturb the soil less. A formula for working out the quantity of water needed is:

$$\text{length} \times \text{width} \times \text{depth (in metres)} \times 7.5$$

Ponds tend to be of irregular dimensions so make allowances for variations in depth and shape. Using a gridded plan can help.

6: Plant up your marginal scheme on all planting zones and naturalise the surrounding area with a native wildflower meadow, trees and shrubs, to create a more diverse habitat.

CREATE A WETLAND BOARDWALK

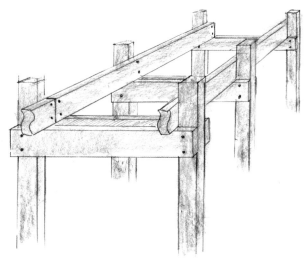

WHY

A raised boardwalk creates a natural crossing if you have areas of boggy or waterlogged ground in your garden. The simplistic design looks at home in a natural scheme.

HOW

1: POSTS

At the correct spacing drive the posts into the ground until firm. Check posts are level and square with boardwalk direction. Ensure posts are at the correct height (these can always be cut later).

2: CROSSBEAM

Attach crossbeams either side of the posts. Ensure these are level and the correct height.

3: STRINGER

Rest the stringer on top of the crossbeams and attach to the post, repeat this on either side and continue the full length of boardwalk.

4: DECKING BOARDS

Fasten decking boards to the stringer using stainless-steel screws. Space decking boards with a 2mm gap to prevent sitting water.

5: RAIL

Use stainless-steel screws to fasten the horizontal rail to the top of upright posts, creating an edge to the boardwalk.

FRAMEWORK
PLAN

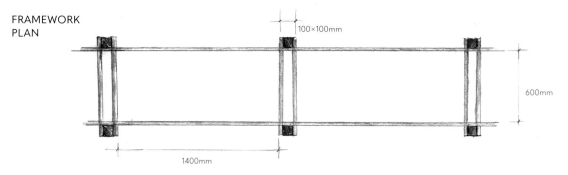

100×100mm

600mm

1400mm

FRAMEWORK
SECTION

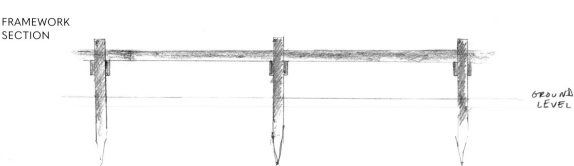

GROUND
LEVEL

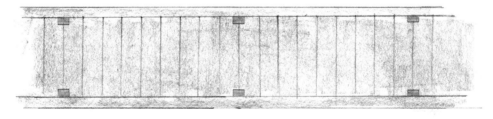

Decking to be cut around post to
provide a seamless detail.

FINAL PLAN with decking and rail

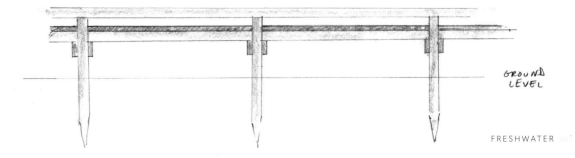

FINAL SECTION with decking and rail

GROUND
LEVEL

'... Jackson plotted a spot on the map and we set off to find it. We ditched the Landrover on a deep, sandy track and carried what we could, and after a while arrived at a tiny beach on the shore of a freshwater lake. We laid our sleeping bags on the sand, toes pointed east, to watch the morning sun ..."

'... We love what we do. It's something we are edlessly passionate about. But for us, it's all about a balanced life. Setting off on adventures with no real aims and very few plans, we always return to work enriched with a deeper connection to nature and a greater understanding of native habitats ...'

PLANTING PRINCIPLES

Planting is multi-layered, a combination of different principles that when combined create atmosphere, movement, balance and structure. For us, it's a lot like painting. Brushstrokes, depth and detail reflect the same attributes as planting. By combining the key principles of planting you can create a unique and stimulating display.

ATMOSPHERE

Atmosphere is the soul of a garden. It is the magical, indefinable quality that has the ability to turn a garden visit into an escape from the outside world.

As designers we seek always to respect the sense of place, choosing plants that blend with the surrounding landscape, for instance. When we try to capture an atmosphere within a garden we are usually seeking to recreate our reaction to a natural habitat we have visited.

Sensitivity to plant selection combined with an awareness of the mercurial qualities of light and the way that a garden can change throughout the day, all play an important part in helping us create an atmospheric space that will sit effortlessly within the wider landscape.

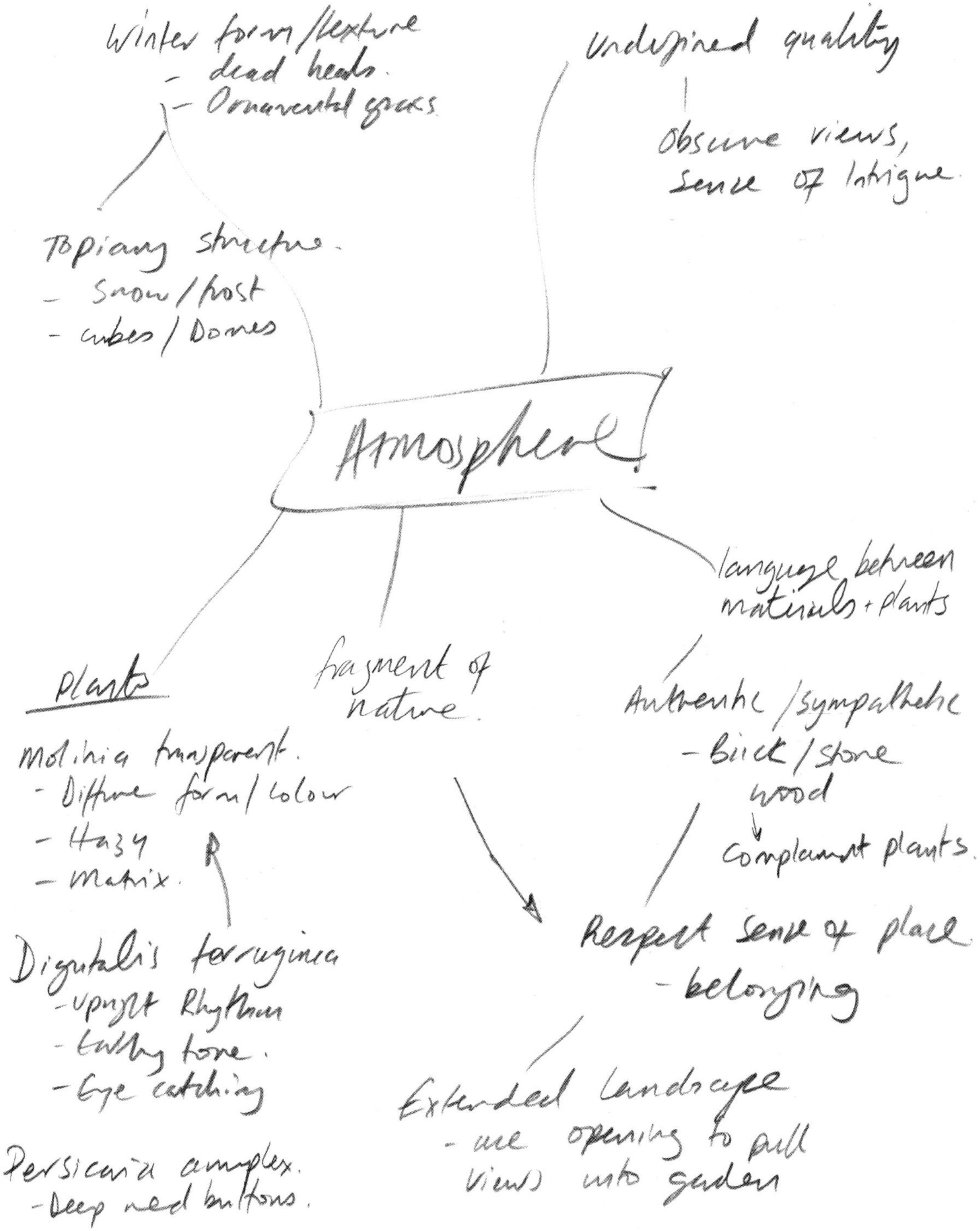

Winter form / texture
- dead heads.
- Ornamental grass.

Undefined quality

obscure views,
sense of Intrigue.

Topiary structure.
- Snow / host
- cubes / Domes

Atmosphere.

language between
materials + plants

Plants

fragment of
nature.

Authentic / sympathetic
- brick / stone
wood
↓
complement plants.

Molinia transparent.
- Diffuse form / colour
- Hazy
- Matrix.

Respect sense of place
- belonging

Digitalis ferruginea
- upright Rhythm
- earthy tone.
- Eye catching

Extended landscape
- use opening to pull
views into garden

Persicaria amplex.
- Deep red buttons.

MOVEMENT

Movement is something we always associate with nature: seasonal changes, for instance, a gentle breeze, the migration of birds.

Grasses and perennials have structures that allow them to sway in a breeze, giving a new sense of life to the garden. Heavy flowerheads often sway to a steady rhythm when touched by the wind, long stems creating the perfect base to rock back and forth upon, and fine-textured seedheads flutter in the softest of breezes. It is the play of these individual rhythms that allows the garden to feel looser and less static.

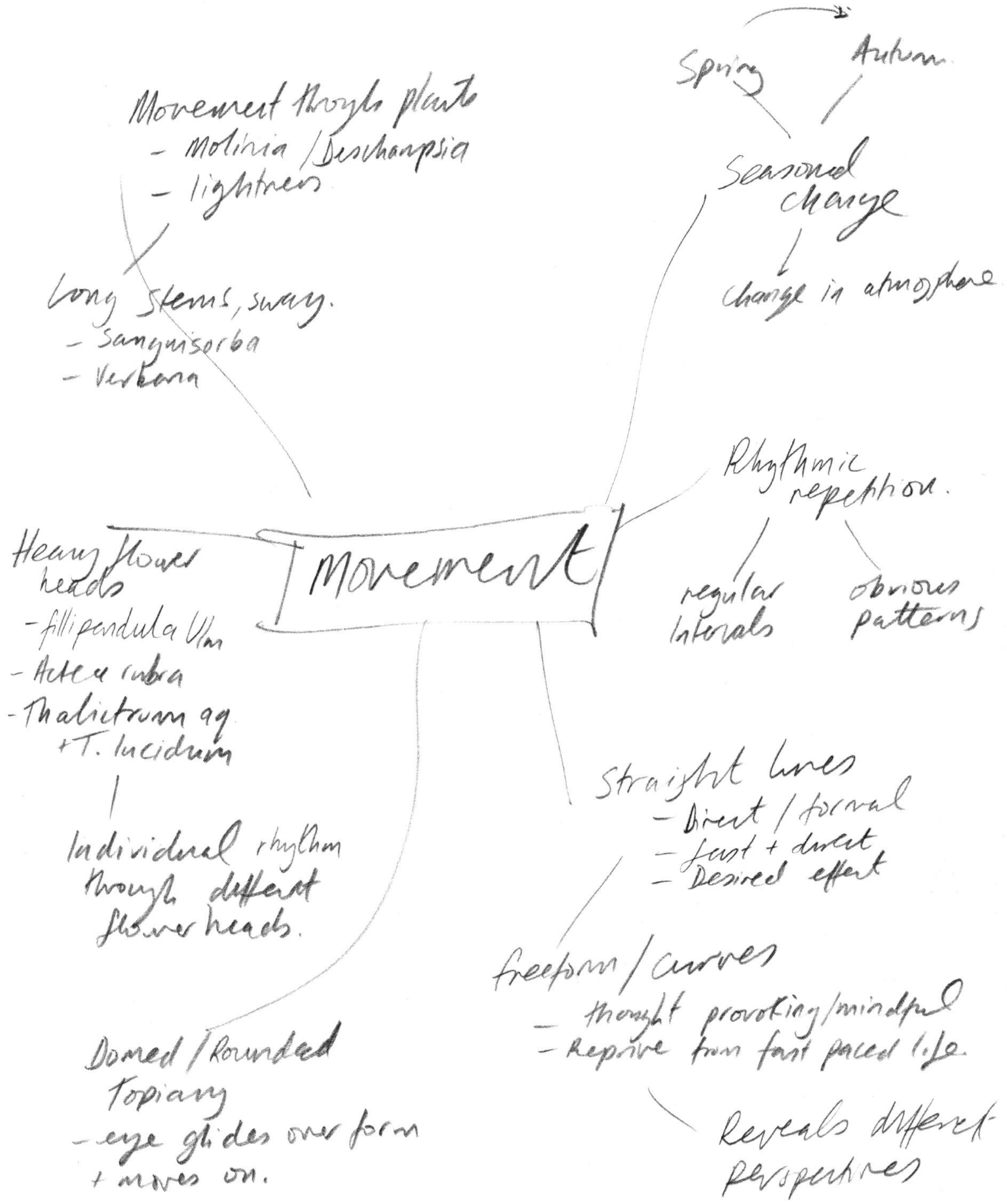

Spring   Autumn

Seasonal
change

change in atmosphere

Movement throws plants
- Molinia / Deschampsia
- lightness

Long stems, sway.
- Sanguisorba
- Verbena

Rhythmic
repetition.

regular   obvious
Intervals   patterns

Heavy flower
heads
- fillipendula Ulm
- Actea rubra
- Thalictrum ag
  +T. lucidum

Individual rhythm
through different
flower heads.

Movement

straight lines
- Direct / formal
- fast + direct
- Desired effect

freeform / curves
- thought provoking/mindful
- Reprive from fast paced life.

Reveals different
perspectives

Domed / Rounded
Topiary
- eye glides over form
+ moves on.

umbellifers.
  - eupatorium P.

plumes.   Dasies.
  - astilbe S.   - Aster. x f.

Globes
  - Phlomis. R

Form + structure.
  - formal
  - natural.

Colour
  - large proportion
    of green.

  - Balanced colour
    Scheme

grasses

↓

Harmony.

Balance

Planting to
balance with
hard landscaping
(even balance)

Proportions
to require the
atmosphere desired

Draws   Between planting
your eye   attributes
level in
specific   - vertical form
directions. - Horizontal
             - transparent + solid.

Repeated forms + colour
creates harmony

BALANCE

Balance creates a sense of harmony and serenity within the garden. There are many different ways of using plants to compose a well-balanced scheme.

Form and repetition play a vital part in controlling and leading the eye. Strong forms such as topiary help to anchor a space, their form static and registering as permanent.

Colour can be delicate and interwoven, become a constantly repeated detail or feature in blocks produced by large, distinctive drifts.

Manipulation of height and structure will determine whether a space feels enclosed or open. A considered approach incorporating these principles will produce a more balanced and harmonious planting scheme.

STRUCTURE

Structure is the underpinning to a planting scheme. Without it the planting runs the risk of merging into a blur. If the shape and form of the selected plants are compatible then harmony results.

Using a bold structural plant such as feather-reed grass allows its rigid vertical nature along with its golden tones to bring a more architectural character to the scheme, obscuring views and creating an element of intrigue. Looser, more relaxed plants will give the illusion of a more formless structure, blurring the division between the planting and the paths.

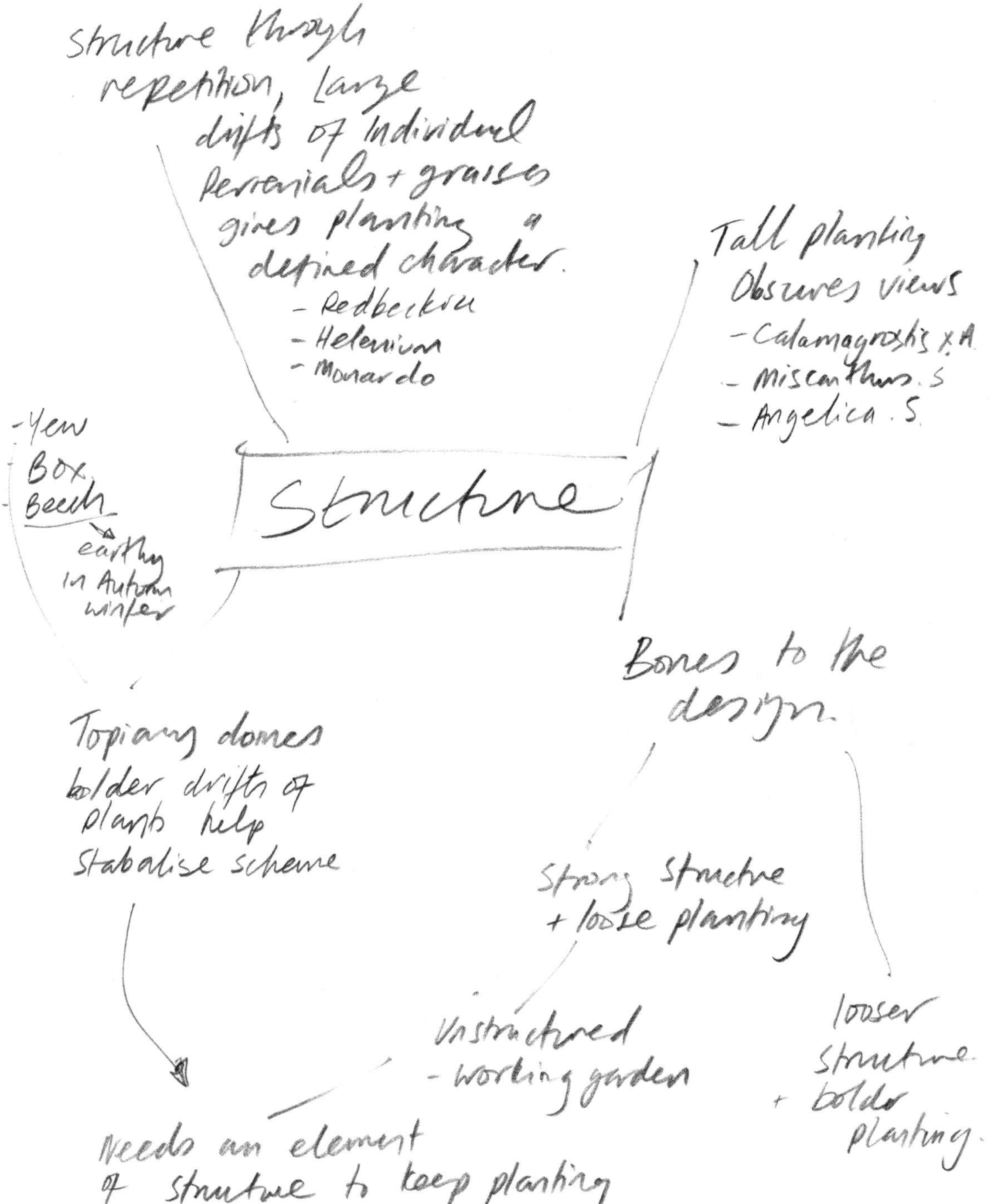

structure through
repetition, Large
drifts of Individual
Perenials + grasses
gives planting "a
defined character.
- Redbeckia
- Helenium
- Monardo

Tall planting
Obscures views
- Calamagrostis x.A
- Miscanthus.S
- Angelica.S.

-Yew
Box.
Beech
earthy
in Autumn
winter

Structure

Bones to the
design.

Topiary domes
bolder drifts of
plants help
stabalise scheme

Strong Structure
+ loose planting

Unstructured
- working garden

looser
structure
+ bolder
planting.

Needs an element
of structure to keep planting
from collaapsing into a tangled mess.

"One of the prettiest and most fragrant of all hedgerow plants"

Meadowsweet
Filipendula ulmaria

PLUMES

Plumes are soft, fluffy flowerheads that sometimes display a subtle transparency. These are neither spires nor umbellifers but act as the middle man, a linking form whose elevated structure provides the perfect outline to catch the eye.

Plumes are more impressive when planted *en masse*, but when more widely scattered they sit confidently amongst their neighbours.

SELECTED PLUMES

Alum root 'White Cloud'
Heuchera sanguinea
'White Cloud'

Chinese fountain grass
Pennisetum alopecuroides

Chinese meadow rue
Thalictrum delavayi
'Album'

False goat's beard 'Deutschland'
Astilbe 'Deutschland'

Dropwort
Filipendula vulgaris

Chestnut-leaved rodgersia
Rodgersia aesculifolia

Meadow sage
Salvia nemorosa
'Schwellenburg'

"Reaching up to two metres, Angelica can cast a supreme shadow over damp places, particularly beside lakes and streams"

Wild angelica
Angelica sylvestris

UMBELLIFERS

Umbrella-like clusters, often associated with native wild flowers such as fennel and fool's parsley, bring a wild naturalism to a garden.

Individual compacted flowers combine to form the flowerhead, creating a horizontal form that contrasts well with the direction of the spires in a planting scheme. Their elegant stems and soft pastel tones allow them to fade off into the mix.

SELECTED UMBELLIFERS

Ice plant
Sedum spectabile
'Stardust'

Atropurpureum
Eupatorium purpureum

Wallich milk parsley
Selinum wallichianum

Buttonsnake root
Eryngium yuccifolium

Yarrow
Achillea millefolium

GLOBES

Their shape is definite, providing a bold display that stands out amongst the softer forms. During winter their round seedheads create dark silhouettes against the faded hues.

En masse globe shapes form a powerful display, creating a strong impression that dominates a planting scheme.

SELECTED GLOBES

Burnet 'Tanna'
Sanguisorba 'Tanna'

Brook thistle
Cirsium rivulare

Turkish sage
Phlomis russeliana

Small globe thistle
Echinops ritro

Bergamot 'Croftway Pink'
Monarda 'Croftway Pink'

Masterwort
Astrantia major

Round-headed garlic
Allium sphaerocephalon

*"Densely packed flowers reveal
a tight, refined shape"*

Rusty foxglove
Digitalis ferruginea

SPIRES

Spires add vertical impact in a garden. Their strict form is fundamental within a planting scheme. They perform best when planted amongst grasses and other perennials where the surrounding plants soften and conceal any rigidity, only accentuating the strong vertical structure as it emerges.

SELECTED SPIRES

Wolf's bane
Aconitum × cammarum
'Grandiflorum Album'

Rusty foxglove
Digitalis ferruginea

White-flowered red bistort
Persicaria
amplexicaulis 'Album'

False indigo
Baptisia
'Dutch Chocolate'

Anise hyssop
Agastache foeniculum

Wood sage
Salvia × sylvestris

Catmint
Nepeta racemosa

Baneberry
Actaea simplex
'White Pearl'

"Iconic daisy petals fall to reveal a bold skeletal form"

Coneflower
Echinacea purpurea

DAISIES

Evocative of wild grasslands, daisies provide a rich and striking display in summer when their seedheads often contrast with the petals, creating a pronounced punctuation mark.

When planted in large drifts and given authority, their bold colour and distinctive shape create a confident rhythm that runs through the planting.

SELECTED DAISIES

Coneflower
Echinacea purpurea

Aster 'Mönch'
Aster × frikartii 'Mönch'

Flat-topped aster
Aster umbellatus

Coneflower
Rudbeckia subtomentosa

Coneflower
Echinacea 'Art's Pride'

Sneezeweed
Helenium 'Moerheim Beauty'

*"Fine plumes catch the slightest breeze,
accentuating the evening light"*

Chinese silver grass
Miscanthus sinensis

GRASSES

Grasses provide motion and connectivity in a planting scheme. Their distinct vertical form is topped with feathery plumes that effortlessly blend with the neighbouring plants.

They can be planted in large drifts or woven poetically amongst perennials. Their versatility and resilient nature add a sense of depth and intrigue to a planting scheme.

SELECTED GRASSES

Korean feather reed grass
Calamagrostis brachytricha

Eulalia
Miscanthus sinensis

Feather grass
Stipa barbata

Moor grass 'Poul Petersen'
Molinia 'Poul Petersen'

Moor grass
Molinia caerulea

Switch grass
Panicum virgatum

Bunny tails
Pennisetum messiacum

THE CHELSEA
FLOWER SHOW

It was always an aspiration to stage a garden at RHS Chelsea. In 2012 we visited the show for the first time, wandered around in awe at all the amazing gardens. How would we get this opportunity? It became part of our 10-year plan. However, the following year, with nothing to lose, we submitted a design; and with a stroke of luck, we managed to get a plot for a small artisan garden. The feeling was incredible, but we realised that opportunities like this don't come around often, so we needed to nail it. We designed a garden called Un Garreg, meaning 'one stone', for which we won a gold. We believed in that garden so much that we would have been gutted to receive anything less, but the feeling of actually getting a gold medal, at Chelsea – nothing beats it.

Once the high of the achievement wore off, we instantly knew that we needed to push for bigger things. As soon as we got back home to Wales, we designed a show

garden for the next year. Again, we were accepted and again, we were hit with a looming realisation of just how pivotal this moment could be in our careers. With the same team and a few crucial extras, we constructed the garden on the corner of the main avenue – a massive contrast to the calm and quiet of the previous year.

We were so proud of this garden; its combination of architecture, stone, soft planting and its wild and rustic approach – though again, we still weren't content. We wanted to push for a full-sized show garden right in the heart of the main avenue, and to contrast our previous rugged approach with a more modern and refined design. This was a chance to really push the boundaries and design something that had never been done before at Chelsea, especially in the company of some of the most renowned names. In 2015, we became the youngest designers to win a gold medal on Main Avenue. Finally, we were content! Well, at least for a while ...

THE CLOUDY BAY GARDEN

RHS CHELSEA GOLD MEDAL 2015

The brief was to create a garden inspired by Cloudy Bay's use of
Pinot noir and Sauvignon blanc.

*"The shack, inspired by Cloudy Bay's original
building back in New Zealand, provided us
with the perfect excuse to incorporate a bit of
architecture. We had never before thought of
putting a moving building in a garden, a detail
that not only created a beautiful sculptural
form but played a unique and pivitol role in
creating an integrated space."*

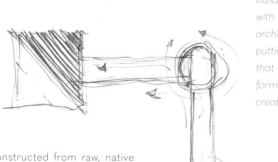

THE SHACK

The shack was constructed from raw, native
materials made in an honest fashion. We
wanted it to complement the garden and blend
organically with the space, not be seen as a
separate element. We wanted to create a piece
of architecture that could adapt, reform and re-
orientate. A translucent sculpture almost, that,
with a change of direction, could become solid
form, constricting views from and into the garden.

*Garden sponsored by Cloudy Bay
in association with Vital Earth*

PINOT NOIR

The red wine inspired the subtlety of the dark tones woven through our planting scheme. These hues created a strong affiliation with the architectural use of oak, infusing the garden with a sense of structure. Dry-stone walls provided a feeling of age and stability and reflected the quality of 'minerality' often found in wine.

SAUVIGNON BLANC

The white wine was approached in the same way. The crispness of the concrete floor seamlessly unrolled through the garden. Its unbroken surface made the space feel lighter and more elegant. The paler planting was understated and delicate, its details acute amidst the layered planting scheme.

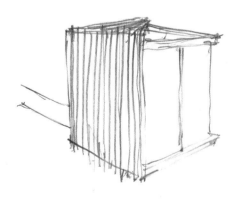

At this orientation the slats positioned on a 45-degree angle create a solid impression.

Seen face on, the linear oak slats provide a glimpse into the shack.

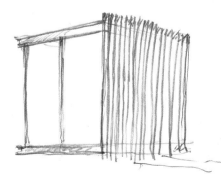

Pete Downey (blacksmith) and Harry looking over the action of the turntable. Pete and his team constructed the entire framework for the garden in his workshop in Pontrilas.

↑ Dad looking over a complete decked walkway. Varied acid washes provided the boards with unique colour distortions

↖ The entire steel framework for the garden with the basic structure of the shack

← Detail of the rails meeting the turntable

Robyn Jones (carpenter) chatting with Harry and Andrew Ball (landscape construction) about the installation of the boundary feature

↑ Steel framework with angled bracing ready to attach decking boards

↖ Robyn, Andy and Harry checking over measurements for the walkway. Acid-washed decking stacked in the background

← Having a lot of fun spraying the galvanised steel sheets for the boundary feature. The spray created a patina that gave the illusion of age

THE CLOUDY BAY GARDEN

Andy, Dad, Nige, Harry, Dave, Tom, Mike and Ade — the Bombay Bad Boys

Rob Morris, master craftsman... never lets the stone get to him!

Amelanchier tree going in

Andrew 'always on the' Ball

Adjusting the turntables

Bells keeping the team sweet ;)

Shack on the track

The chain gang

THE NIGHT SKY GARDEN

RHS CHELSEA SILVER GILT MEDAL 2014

Inspired by the dark-sky status that was awarded to the Brecon Beacons, this
garden was designed to respect the natural beauty of the National Park.

A network of cobbled paths meanders through a tapestry
of soft, fluid planting, its tones inspired by the Milky Way
that at night provides a luminous spectacle overhead.

Two large moon pools catch images of the night sky, reflecting the stars and connecting the garden to the heavens.

A grassy bowl donates a perfect spot to sit, connected to
and yet out of the elements.

Stone walls define the garden, their serpentine form
intriguing, while large boulders positioned at the edges of
the pathways lend a sense of age and mystery.

*"This garden was very important to us. Growing up
in Brecon we took for granted the clear starry nights.
It was a chance to pay homage to a place that has
been a huge inspiration."*

Garden sponsored by Vital Earth

ACKNOWLEDGEMENTS

Writing this book has been a really special moment in our lives. There have been a lot of long days and late nights, but we've had so much fun throughout the whole process. Without the people involved helping us along the way, this book wouldn't have been possible.

Firstly, we'd love to thank Ajda Vučićević who has been a great laugh and an absolute pleasure to work alongside, as well as everyone at Penguin Random House, especially Becky Millar, for keeping us on track.

We'd also like to thank Tim Barnes for dealing with our frequent layout requests :) – thanks for the justified text! Lizzy Barlow Brown and Lizzy Morgan from James Grant Management have been with us all the way, and of course, Rory Scarfe – thanks for doing the deal!

Without the BBC we wouldn't be in the position we are to write this book, so we'd like to thank Alex McLeod for commissioning *Garden Rescue*, and everyone else who has been a part of the series.

INDEX

Page references in *italics* indicate photographs and illustrations.

PHOTOGRAPHIC ACKNOWLEDGEMENTS

Every reasonable effort has been made to contact all copyright holders but if there are any errors or omissions, we will insert the appropriate acknowledgement in subsequent printings of this book.

All sketches and designs are authors' own.

AL = Alamy   F = Flickr   IS= iStock   WK = Wikimedia Commons

INTRODUCTION
Authors' own

PRINCIPLES OF DESIGN:
p.6 © IS

ELEMENTS OF DESIGN:
p.20 © IS

WOODLAND
pp.30–31, 34, 35, 36, 37, 38, 40, 41, 58 © IS
p.73 Authors' own

Plant listings and Meadow Mix (alphabetical order):

Acer campestre © Willow, CC BY-SA 2.5 via WK
Actaea simplex © Alpsdake, CC BY-SA 3.0 via WK
Agrostemma githago © IS
Ajuga reptans © IS
Alnus glutinosa, © Bruce Marlin, CC BY-SA 3.0 via WK
Amelanchier lamarckii © Jean Van Schaftingen, CC BY-SA 4.0, via WK
Aster divaricatus © Me, CC BY-2.5 via WK
Astrantia major 'Alba' © Howard Mackay CC BY 3.0 via WK
Athyrium filix-femina © MurielBendel, CC BY-SA 4.0, via WK
Betula pendula,© Percita CC BY-SA 2.0 via WK
Betula pubescens ©Willow, CC BY-SA 3.0 via WK
Briza media © Bartosz Cuber CC BY-SA 3.0 via WK
Buxus sempervirens © Sannicolasdeugarte, CC BY-SA 3.0 via WK
Cornus sanguinea © Hans Hillewaert, CC BY-SA 4.0 via WK
Corylus avellana contorta © SB Johnny, CC BY-SA 3.0 via WK
Crataegus monogyna © H. Zell, CC BY-SA 3.0 via WK
Cynosurus cristatus © Hans Hillewaert, CC BY-SA 4.0, via WK
Deschampsia cespitosa © Christian Fischer, CC BY-SA 3.0 via WK
Digitalis lutea © Bernd Haynold, CC-BY-SA-3.0 via WK
Dryopteris filix-mas © Valérie75, CC-BY-SA-3.0 via WK
Fagus sylvatica 'Grandidentata' © Jean-Pol Grandmot, CC BY 3.0 via WK
Festuca rubra © IS
Geranium phaeum 'Samobor' © Wouterhagens, public domain, via WK
Hakonechloa macra © Steffen Hauser / botanikfoto / A
Hamamelis mollis © Donar Reiskoffer, CC BY 3.0, via WK
Hedera helix © Sannicolasdeugarte, CC BY-SA 3.0 via WK
Hyacinthoides non-scripta © Peter O'Connor, CC BY-SA 2.0 via F
Ilex crenata © SB Johnny CC-BY-SA-3.0 via WK
Kirengeshoma palmata © I, KENPEI, CC-BY-SA-3.0 via WK
Ligustrum ovalifolium © MPF CC-BY-SA-3.0 via WK
Luzula nivea © Megan Hansen, CC BY-SA 2.0 via F
Prunus 'Accolade' © Derek Ramsey, CC-BY-SA-3.0 via WK
Rhododendrum 'Cunningham White' © Ulf Eliasson, CC BY-SA 3.0, via WK
Sambucus nigra © Franz Xaver, CC BY-SA 3.0 via WK
Sphagnum © IS
Taxus baccata © IS
Tellima grandiflora © Hedwig Storch, CC BY-SA 3.0, via WK
Viburnum lantana © Meneerke Bloem, CC BY-SA 4.0 via WK

GRASSLAND
p.74–5, 78, 80–88, 90–91, 102–103, 116–17 © IS
p.76–77, 91, 118–19 © Authors' own

Plant listings and Meadow Mix (alphabetical order):

Achillea millefolium © Dcrjsr, CC BY-SA 3.0 via WK CC BY-SA
Agastache foeniculum © IS
Allium sphaerocephalon © Mike Peel, CC BY-SA 4.0 via WK
Anthriscus sylvestris © Qwert1234, CC BY-SA 3.0 via WK
Aster × frikartii 'Monch' © Dominicus Johannes Bergsma, CC BY-SA 3.0 via WK
Aster 'Monte Casino' © Calin Darabus CC BY 2.0 via F
Briza media © Hajotthu, CC BY-SA 3.0 via WK
Deschampsia cespitosa © IS
Deschampsia flexuosa © Franz Xaver, CC BY-SA 3.0 via WK
Echinacea purpurea 'White Swan' © Andrej Korzun CC BY-SA 4.0 via WK
Filipendula ulmaria © Hans Hillewaert CC BY-SA 4.0 via WK
Helenium 'Moerheim Beauty' [Asteraceae] © Willow, CC BY-SA 3.0, via WK
Melica ciliata © Javier Martin, CC BY-SA 3.0 via WK
Miscanthus sinensis var gracillimus © I, KENPEI, CC-BY-SA-3.0 via WK
Monarda 'Squaw' © IS
Monarda didyma 'Croftway Pink' © Andrej Korzun, CC BY-SA 3.0 via WK
Panicum virgatum © Daderot, Public domain, via WK

Pennisetum alopecuroides © Tubifex, CC BY-SA 3.0, via WK
Persicaria amplexicaulis 'Firetail' © Daderot, Public domain, via WK
Phlomis tuberosa 'Amazone' © IS
Rudbeckia hirta © Joshua Mayer, CC BY-SA 3.0 via Flickr
Rudbeckia subtomentosa © Derek Ramsey, CC BY-SA 2.5, via WK
Sanguisorba officinalis © H. Zell CC BY-SA 3.0, via WK
Stipa barbata © Daderot, Public domain, via WK
Stipa calamagrostis © Zena Elea / AL

COASTAL
pp.120–21, 126–133, 140, 148–9, 152, 159, 162, 164 © IS
pp.166–7 © Authors' own

Plant listings and Meadow Mix (alphabetical order):

Achillea millefolium © Paul Asman and Jill Lenoble, CC BY 2.0, via F
Agrostis stolonifera © Matt Lavin, CC BY-SA 2, via WK
Alchemilla mollis © By Anneli Salo, CC BY-SA 3.0, via WK
Alnus glutinosa © Luis Fernández García, CC BY-SA 3.0, via WK
Festuca glauca 'Elijah Blue' © IS
Calamagrostis × acutiflora 'Karl Foerster' © Daryl Mitchell, CC BY-SA 2.0 via WK
Centranthus ruber © Wouter Hagens, Public domain, via WK
Chasmanthium latifolium © Averater, CC BY 4.0, via WK
Crambe cordifolia © Rasbak, CC-BY-SA-3.0, via WK
Crataegus monogyna © Franz Xaver, CC BY-SA 3.0, via WK
Cupressus macrocarpa © vera46, CC BY 2.0 via WK
Echinops bannaticus © Pethan, CC-BY-SA-3.0, via WK
Festuca pratensis © T.Voekler, CC BY-SA 3.0, via WK
Festuca rubra © Bildoj, CC BY-SA 3.0, via WK
Helictotrichon sempervirens © Matt Lavin, CC BY-SA 2.0, via WK
Holcus lanatus © Franz Xaver, CC BY-SA 3.0, via WK
Laurus nobilis © By H. Zell, CC BY-SA 3.0, via WK
Lotus corniculatus © IS
Miscanthus nepalensis © katewarn images / AL
Pennisetum alopecuroides 'Hameln' © André Karwath, CC BY-SA 2.5, via WK
Phlomis russeliana © Georges Jansoone, Public domain, via WK
Pinus nigra cone © Roberto Verzo, CC BY 2.0, via WK
Pittosporum tobira © Jean-Pol Grandmont, CC BY 3.0, via WK
Plantago major © Rasbak, CC-BY-SA-3.0, via WK
Poa nemoralis © James Lindsey, Ecology of Commanster CC BY-SA 2.5, via WK
Quercus ilex © Jean-Pol Grandmont, CC BY-SA 3.0, via WK
Rosmarinus officinalis © THOR, CC BY 2.0, via WK
Scabiosa columbaria © Stan Shebs, CC BY-SA 3.0, via WK
Schizachyrium scoparium © Krzysztof Ziarnek, CC BY-SA 4.0, via WK
Sedum 'Autumn Joy' © Magnus Manske, CC BY-SA 3.0, via WK
Silene dioica © IS
Stachys byzantina © Frank Vincentz, CC-BY-SA-3.0, via WK
Tamarix ramosissima © Jerzy Opioła, CC-BY-SA-3.0, via WK
Verbascum bombyciferum 'Polarsommer' © Stickpen, Public Domain, via WK

MOUNTAIN
p.168–9, 171–6, 178–179, 194–5, 214–5 © IS
p.202 © LOOK Die Bildagentur der Fotografen GmbH / AL

Plant listings and Meadow Mix (alphabetical order):

Achillea clavennae © Enrico Blasutto, CC BY-SA 3.0, via WK
Amelanchier canadensis © I, KENPEI, CC-BY-SA-3.0, via WK
Anemone japonica © ChickenFreak, Public domain, via WK
Aquilegia vulgaris © BerndH, CC BY-SA 3.0, via WK
Artemisa 'Powis Castle' © Patrick Standish, CC BY 2.0, via F
Calluna vulgaris © IS
Carex divulsa © Javier martin, Public domain, via WK
Carex buchananii © Stickpen, Public domain, via WK
Digitalis purpurea © Nevit Dilmen, CC BY-SA 3.0, via WK
Festuca paniculata © IS
Hebe buchananii 'Minor' © GFK-Flora / AL
Iberis sempervirens © Heron2, via WK
Linum Suffruticosum © Javier martin, Public domain, via WK
Miscanthus sinensis 'Morning Light' © Zoonar GmbH / AL
Miscanthus sinensis 'Kleine Silberspinne' © Manfred Werner, CC BY-SA 3.0, via WK
Nepeta faassenii 'Six Hills Giant' © Wouter Hagens, Public domain, via WK
Pennisetum orientale © Cillas, CC BY-SA 4.0, via WK
Penstemon pinifolius © Andy king50, CC BY-SA 3.0, via WK
Penstemon 'Raven' © Martin Hughes-Jones / AL
Perovskia atriplicifolia © Wouter Hagens, Public domain, via WK
Persicaria affinis 'Darjeeling Red' © John Tann, CC BY 2.0, via WK
Pinus sylvestris © Crusier, CC BY 3.0, via WK

Poa labillardieri © Florapix / AL
Poplus alba © Dimitar Nàydenov, CC BY-SA 3.0, via WK
Primula vulgaris © IS
Prunus spinosa © Isidre Blanc, CC BY-SA 3.0, via WK
Rhododendron impeditum © Daderot, public domain, via WK
Rosa rugosa © Kamil Porembinski, CC BY-SA 2.0, via WK
Rumex acetosa © Ivar Leidus CC BY-SA 3.0, via WK
Salix purpurea © Sten, CC-BY-SA-3.0, via WK
Salvia greggii © Stan Shebs, CC BY-SA 3.0, via WK
Saxifraga × urbium © I, Hugo.arg, CC BY-SA 3.0 via WK
Sorbus aucuparia © Simon A. Eugster, CC BY-SA 3.0, via WK
Stachys byzantina © Stan Shebs, CC BY-SA 3.0, via WK
Stipa enuissima © Dinkum, Public Domain, via WK
Viburnum dentatum © Vojtěch Zavadil, CC BY-SA 3.0, via WK
Poplus alba © Dimitar Nàydenov, CC BY-SA 3.0, via WK

FRESHWATER

pp.216–8, 220–24, 226–7, 242 © IS
pp.235, 260–1 © Authors' own
p.249 © AL

Plant listings and Meadow Mix (alphabetical order):

Alnus incana © Vassil, Public domain, via WK
Angelica sylvestris © IS
Aponogeton distachyos © Chiyako92 CC BY-SA 3.0, via WK
Betula nigra © IS
Cephalanthus occidentalis © Rufino Osorio, CC BY-SA 2.5, via WK
Darmera peltata © RBflora / AL
Eriophorum angustifolium © Franz Xaver, CC BY-SA 3.0, via WK
Eupatorium cannabinum © IS
Hottonia palustris © Olivier Pichard, CC BY-SA 3.0, via WK
Ilex decidua © Nature photography by Victoria Krasnoshchekova / AL
Iris pseudacorus © Aiwok, CC BY-SA 3.0, via WK
Ligularia przewalskii © Andrej Korzun, CC BY-SA 3.0, via WK
Marsilea quadrifolia © Show_ryu, CC BY-SA 3.0, via WK
Myosotis scorpioides © I, KENPEI, CC-BY-SA-3.0, via WK
Myriophyllum spicata © IS
Nymphaea alba © Валасенко, CC BY-SA 3.0, via WK
Osmunda regalis © IS
Phalaris arundinacea © Rasbak, CC BY-SA 3.0, via WK
Poa trivialis © By Rasbak, CC-BY-SA-3.0, via WK
Potamogeton crispus © Aroche, CC BY-SA 2.5, via WK
Prunus padus © Pollo, CC BY 3.0, via WK
Ranunculus aquatilis © Hans Hillewaert, CC BY-SA 4.0, via WK
Rhamnus frangula © Frank Vincentz, CC-BY-SA-3.0, via WK
Rodgersia podophylla © Dalgial, CC BY 3.0, via WK
Sagittaria graminea © peganum, CC BY-SA 2.0, via WK
Salix caprea © Willow, CC BY-SA 2.5, via WK
Sanguisorba minor © Fornax, CC BY-SA 3.0, via WK
Sanguisorba officinalis © IS
Saururus cernuus © Fritzflohrreynolds, CC BY-SA 3.0, via WK
Typha angustifolia © Petr Filippov, CC BY-SA 2.5, via WK
Viburnum opulus © gailhampshire, CC BY 2.0, via WK

PLANTING PRINCIPLES

p.262 © Moët Hennessey UK, Cloudy Bay Garden 2015
    taken by Phill Williams
p.264 © Rex May / AL
p.266 © Alex Ramsay / AL
p.269 © Martin Hughes-Jones / AL
p.270 © John Glover / AL
p.271 © Authors' own
pp.274, 276, 279–80, 283 © IS

CHELSEA FLOWER SHOW

p.284 © Gary Morrisroe
p.288–290 © Authors' own
pp.291–3 © Moët Hennessey UK, Cloudy Bay Garden 2015
    taken by Phill Williams
p.295 © Rachel Warne
pp.296–7 © Authors' own

ACKNOWLEDGEMENTS

Photograph: Authors' own

LEGAL NOTE

Please find link to Creative Commons Licenses used:
CC BY-SA: 4.0 https://creativecommons.org/licenses/by-sa/4.0/legalcode
CC BY-SA 3.0: https://creativecommons.org/licenses/by-sa/3.0/legalcode
CC BY 3.0: https://creativecommons.org/licenses/by/3.0/legalcode
CC BY-SA 2.5: https://creativecommons.org/licenses/by-sa/2.5/legalcode
CC BY 2.0: https://creativecommons.org/licenses/by/2.0/legalcode
CC BY-SA 2.0: https://creativecommons.org/licenses/by-sa/2.0/legalcode
Public Domain: https://creativecommons.org/publicdomain/zero/1.0/

CENTURY

20 Vauxhall Bridge Road
London SW1V 2SA

Century is part of the Penguin Random House group of companies
whose addresses can be found at global.penguinrandomhouse.com.

Penguin
Random House
UK

First published in 2017 by Century

www.penguin.co.uk

A CIP catalogue record for this book is available
from the British Library.

ISBN 978 1 7808 9741 7
Love Your Plot

Designed and typset in Quasimoda 8/13pt by
Tim Barnes ℞ chicken, herechickychicky.com

Colour separations by BORN
Printed and bound in China by C&C Offset Printing Co. Ltd.

Penguin Random House is committed to a sustainable future
for our business, our readers and our planet. This book is made from
Forest Stewardship Council® certified paper.